LANGUAGE AND LITERACY SERIES

Dorothy S. Strickland, FOUNDING EDITOR
Celia Genishi and Donna E. Alvermann, SERIES EDITORS
ADVISORY BOARD: Richard Allington, Kathryn Au, Bernice Cullinan, Colette Daiute,
Anne Haas Dyson, Carole Edelsky, Mary Juzwik, Susan Lytle, Django Paris, Timothy Shanahan

continued

For volumes in the NCRLL Collection (edited by JoBeth Allen and Donna E. Alvermann) and the Practitioners Bookshelf Series
(edited by Celia Genishi and Donna E. Alvermann), as well as other titles in this series, please visit www.tcpress.com.

The Teacher-Writer

Creating Writing Groups
for Personal and Professional Growth

Christine M. Dawson

Foreword by Robert P. Yagelski

NATIONAL WRITING PROJECT

TEACHERS COLLEGE PRESS

TEACHERS COLLEGE | COLUMBIA UNIVERSITY
NEW YORK AND LONDON

Published simultaneously by Teachers College Press, 1234 Amsterdam Avenue, New York, NY 10027 and National Writing Project, 2105 Bancroft Way, Berkeley, CA 94720-1042.

Through its mission, the National Writing Project (NWP) focuses the knowledge, expertise, and leadership of our nation's educators on sustained efforts to help youth become successful writers and learners. NWP works in partnership with local Writing Project sites, located on nearly 200 university and college campuses, to provide high-quality professional development in schools, universities, libraries, museums, and after-school programs. NWP envisions a future where every person is an accomplished writer, engaged learner, and active participant in a digital, interconnected world.

Cover design by adam c. bohannon. Photo by silver-john / Adobe Stock.

Chapter 2 contains reworkings of material originally published in Dawson, Robinson, Hanson, VanRiper, & Ponzio, Creating a Breathing Space: An Online Teachers' Writing Group, *English Journal*, 102(3), 93–99. Copyright 2013 by the National Council of Teachers of English. Used by permission.

"Fire" is from *A Leader's Guide to Reflective Practice* by Judy Brown, Trafford Press. Copyright 2006 by Judy Brown. Used by permission.

Library of Congress Cataloging-in-Publication Data

Names: Dawson, Christine M.
Title: The teacher-writer : creating writing groups for personal and
  professional growth / Christine M. Dawson; foreword by Robert P. Yagelski.
Description: New York, NY : Teachers College Press, 2016. | Series: Language
  and literacy series | Includes bibliographical references and index.
Identifiers: LCCN 2016037361| ISBN 9780807758007 (pbk.)
Subjects: LCSH: Authorship. | Authorship—Collaboration. | Teachers.
Classification: LCC PN145 .D39 2016 | DDC 808.02—dc23
LC record available at https://lccn.loc.gov/2016037361

ISBN 978-0-8077-5800-7 (paper)
ISBN 978-0-8077-7510-3 (ebook)

Printed on acid-free paper
Manufactured in the United States of America

24 23 22 21 20 19 18 17   8 7 6 5 4 3 2 1

*For **Becca***
May you always find space in your life for writing,
and may your life be filled with teachers who are as
thoughtful and creative as those featured in this book.

*And for **Karen, Nell, Jillian,** and **Christina,***
my inspirational writing group friends.

Contents

Foreword

For more than 2 decades I have taught in two university teacher education programs that lead to a certification to teach English in secondary schools. Most of the hundreds of students I have been privileged to work with in those programs were earnest, academically successful, and genuinely committed to becoming good English teachers. They were also avid readers. In fact, most of them wanted to become English teachers in large part because of their passion for literature and their sincere belief that they could impart to their future students the same appreciation for the value—and joy—of reading literary works that they themselves had. Almost none of them, however, saw themselves as writers. Few wrote at all outside of their classes, and many admitted a fear of writing. These facts would be unremarkable except for the related fact that almost all of these teachers-in-training would, once they began teaching in middle and high schools, be assigned the critical responsibility of teaching their adolescent students to write.

This state of affairs—that so many English teachers in the United States do not see themselves as writers, despite their responsibility for teaching writing—makes the publication of Christine Dawson's engaging book, *The Teacher-Writer: Creating Writing Groups for Personal and Professional Growth*, significant. If nothing else, Dawson's work shines a desperately needed light on the potential importance of writing in the professional and personal lives of teachers—most importantly, those who teach the nation's children to write. In that respect alone, Dawson has made a valuable contribution to the ongoing discussions about literacy instruction, teacher education, and school improvement.

Dawson's book gives us an in-depth look at how writing figures into the work, the identities, and the complex private lives of five teachers, one of whom is Dawson herself. Through her intimate portraits of these teachers and her careful analysis of their writing experiences, Dawson illuminates the transformative potential of writing as a way to make sense of our lives and engage deeply with the world around us. She shows us how these teachers, through their shared experiences as writers, gained a profound understanding of the capacity of writing to help them navigate the challenges of contemporary life. This understanding not only enables them to use writing as a tool for living their own lives, but also informs their ways of thinking about teaching writing, which has the potential to transform the lives of their students.

Especially significant is Dawson's effort in this book to "focus less on how to 'be a writer' and instead consider how we might purposefully 'do writing'—in whatever ways it works in our lives," as she writes in Chapter 1. In making this shift, Dawson challenges prevailing—and limited—conceptions of writing that emphasize the production of sanctioned texts; instead, she embraces a richer, more nuanced understanding of writing not only as a social practice but also as an epistemic and ontological act. This view of writing, which emerges from her theoretical assumptions, as well as her careful reflection on her experiences as a writer and those of her study participants, makes it possible for her to find genuine value in writing that, by conventional standards, may seem mundane but actually serves powerful purposes in the lives of the teachers we meet in this book. In this regard, Dawson provides compelling examples of acts of writing as knowing and being rather than exclusively as textual production. Her book thus contributes empirical support for an emerging alternative to the utilitarian conception of writing that continues to inform instruction in the nation's schools and the efforts to reform it.

Most of all, however, this is a very practical book that offers teachers—or anyone interested in writing—a useful guide for engaging in and sustaining writing as an individual and social practice. In examining the experiences of the teachers in her study as they write in the context of their writing group, Dawson offers a tangible vision of how a writing group might function. Her analysis of her group's experiences and the lists of concrete suggestions in each chapter make this book an eminently useful guide for those seeking to create and sustain a writing group that can become an integral part of their writing lives. Perhaps most important, Dawson vividly shows us how teachers can overcome the many obstacles they face in trying to make writing a substantive professional and personal practice. More than anything else about this book, these practical suggestions can help teachers become *writers*—in the rich, multifaceted way that Dawson understands that term.

—Robert P. Yagelski
University at Albany, State University of New York
June, 2016

Preface

As writing teachers, we are constantly encouraged to *"be* writers" ourselves. But what does that look like? How can we create space for our own writing, amid all the other demands associated with our profession? This book helps show teachers that pursuing writing projects is both worthwhile and realistic. Chapter by chapter, this book provides teachers with strategies to help get started on projects, build energy for writing, overcome obstacles, create support systems using online technology, and develop coherence across their writing lives.

The Teacher-Writer meets teachers wherever they are in their writing and teaching development—whether as novice teachers just beginning to pursue writing, as teachers emerging from a professional development experience that has sparked a new interest in writing (perhaps a writing retreat, graduate course, or National Writing Project summer institute), or as experienced writers seeking support in furthering their development. This book provides a view of what is possible, particularly when working within a collaborative group to create the time and space for writing. It offers useful writing group routines, methods to adapt writing communities to online settings (critical for teachers who are separated geographically from other interested colleagues), discussions of common obstacles teacher-writers face, questions that can frame collaborative inquiry, and rich examples of conversations and texts shared in meetings of an actual online teacher writing group.

This book also helps teachers reimagine what it may look like to be a teacher-writer. It provides multiple views of different teacher-writers in action, illustrating a range of strategies, commitments, and interests. Rather than offering a prescriptive account of "right" ways of being teacher-writers, this book uses examples of real teachers' writing and talk to show the value of participating within a community of writers over time. Across the examples in this book, teacher-writers are inventing—ways to write, ways to use writing to work through challenges and shape relationships, ways to sustain energy for writing, and ways to reclaim even workplace texts as their own. Highlighting the inventive work of teacher-writers, this book considers our writing practices as central to our intellectual and creative lives, and it offers resources to enable teachers to pursue personal and professional writing fulfillment.

The following questions, informed by a theoretical framework of invention, guide this inquiry into teachers as writers:

- How do teacher-writers in a writing group work within and against constraints to create and develop writing projects?
- What else, besides written texts, do teacher-writers compose through participation in a writing group?
- How do teacher-writers in a writing group use and adapt writing strategies across contexts?
- How do the various "outcomes" of teacher-writers' invention shape writing experiences and writing group meetings?

This book focuses on the teacher-writer as a whole person, who may write for multiple purposes and audiences and who may participate in varied ways in a writing group. While there are many things this book can and does explore, it is just as important to consider what it does not set out to do. This book does not seek to trace the development of any particular text over time (where the focus may be on textual production) or to follow a teacher-writer's use of particular writing pedagogies (where the focus may be on teaching techniques). Rather, I foreground teachers' creativity as they collaborate to compose many things beyond texts and classroom practices.

Additionally, I do not intend to present a model of a writing group that should be replicated exactly in a different context or with different participants ("meet twice a month, add talk, and stir"). The featured writing group would, of course, look different with different writers, and the group experience would change if any member were to leave or if another writer were to join. This book presents a close look at people talking and writing together over time and through respectful collaboration to illustrate possible ways writing groups may evolve. I include overviews of strategies, suggestions, and guiding questions to support other teacher-writers who seek to develop their own writing practices and writing group experiences.

Chapter 1 introduces the book, foregrounding the creativity of teacher-writers and introducing some of the benefits and challenges we may experience as we pursue our own writing. Chapter 2 then provides logistical information about how teacher-writers might set up a writing group, including negotiating core commitments, creating meeting routines, and, if they wish, using online technologies.

Chapters 3 through 7 present clusters of strategies developed and adapted by teacher-writers as they craft texts and writing practices. Each chapter illustrates these techniques through examples of talk and texts shared by actual teacher-writers during writing group meetings, and each chapter concludes with a list of primary strategies and guiding questions. Finally, Chapter 8 provides an opportunity to look across and beyond the book, to highlight ways teacher-writers may use and adapt strategies as they develop writing practices and identities.

Acknowledgments

Several years ago, amid the intense demands of starting their first teaching jobs, four women joined with me to form an online writing group. It has been an honor to share writing with them, every 2 weeks, since then. They have inspired me as a writer and as a teacher, and their creativity, humor, honesty, and courage are reflected on every page of this book. Nell, Christina, Karen, and Jillian, I am forever grateful. I have learned so much from each of you.

This book emerged from my study of our first, formative year as a writing group. I was fortunate to have Mary Juzwik, Julie Lindquist, Marilyn Wilson, and Janine Certo among my mentors and first readers of this work; they shared literature and advice, perspective and imagination. Their thoughtful feedback shaped this project (and me) in important ways. I am also grateful for the feedback from my colleagues Anny Fritzen Case, Ann Lawrence, and Deborah Vriend Van Duinen, who also read and responded to this work across many stages. In the moments when I could not see my next step, I trusted their eyes and their judgment. They never let me down. Ann Lawrence also provided me with a wonderful model of how to organize a wiki for our writing group, which was immensely helpful. Additionally, I am grateful to Bob Yagelski for his mentorship and for writing the foreword to this book, and to Anne Elrod Whitney, Leah Zuidema, Jim Fredricksen, Arthur Applebee, Judith Langer, Anne Haas Dyson, Peter Smagorinsky, and Michael Sherry, each of whom has helped me grow in significant ways as a writer and as a researcher.

The process of moving a study into a book has proved to be a complex one, and I am indebted to Emily Spangler, Acquisitions Editor at Teachers College Press, for her guidance and support over the past several years. She read sample chapters and overviews, answered countless questions, and talked me through every step of this process. Her feedback and vision have shaped this book in significant ways. It is also a rare gift when writing a book-length manuscript to have someone else read it in entirety. Thank you to Alison Daltroy, Development Editor, whose questions and insights brought clarity and focus across the manuscript, and to all the others at Teachers College Press who supported this endeavor, especially Kathy Caveney, Lori Tate, and Jamie Rasmussen. Thank you also to Cara

Dempsey, who read every chapter (often multiple times), offering feedback and, most critically, allowing me the luxury of discussing the themes and details of the book with a fellow writer and teacher.

Finally, my family and friends have been my most constant support system. My parents, John and Eileen, and my brother, Mark, through their example and love, opened doors to literacy and helped me embrace a life of learning. Thank you for always believing in me. My husband, Eric, and daughter, Becca, have been my constant companions throughout this journey. Thank you for helping me keep things in perspective and for giving me the time to write. I simply could not have done this without you. Thank you for always making me smile, and thank you to Becca for reminding me how magical it is to be an author.

The Teacher-Writer

Why Write?

To be a teacher-writer is different than being a teacher or being a writer. It is to be one who both engages a process of composing and one who engages others in doing so. It is both to guide students and to work alongside them.

—Anne Elrod Whitney,
"And Yet We Write: Being a Teacher-Writer" (2013)

"The main reason I joined, to be honest, was because I wanted to talk with you all," Karen admits. Pausing briefly, she continues, "But another reason would be, like, I was so used to doing academic writing. And I had never really tried writing for *myself*. Well, not never, but I didn't frequently write for myself, so I thought this would be a good opportunity to do that."

Our writing group is gathered together on a Thursday evening, a little more than a year after we started meeting. We are five teacher-writers spread across several states, each of us at our own computer in our own home as we reflect on our work together. We ask ourselves: How had we created this writing group, an opportunity to gather and talk every 2 weeks about our writing and our writing lives? What have we each gained from the experience? And why are we still going strong? Our online conversation via Skype (free, online conference call program) is lively and personal, as we revisit moments and realizations from the past year. In many ways we celebrate what we have invented together: texts we are proud of, a writing group we enjoy, relationships we have developed across distance and teaching contexts, and ways of being writers amid the busy work of teaching.

The significance of teachers' writing practices, which lies at the heart of this book, has been demonstrated across several decades of research and practice. When teachers engage in reflective, process-oriented writing practices, they are better able to use their own experiences to inform pedagogy, respond to students' needs, empathize with student writers, and provide classroom models at different stages of composition (Dahl, 1992; Gillespie, 1985; Kittle, 2008; Murray, 1968). Writing also helps teachers inquire into and share teaching practices with other professionals (Hicks et al., 2013; McEntee, 1998; Robbins, Seaman, Yancey, & Yow, 2006; Whitney et al., 2012; Whitney et al., 2014).

Yet teachers' writing can offer much more than service to their students or profession. As teachers, we are whole, complex people, who exist both within and beyond our public and professional roles. When Karen spoke of her reasons for joining our writing group, she did not discuss her dedication to her students or profession (although I can attest she has both). She joined our writing group out of a sincere interest to explore other possibilities for writing in her life and to build relationships with other teacher-writers.

This chapter provides an introduction to some of the benefits and challenges teacher-writers may experience. I begin by exploring the nature of writing itself, using the concept of *invention* to consider the active, social, and experiential aspects of writing practices. This chapter then explores what other teachers have said about the role of writing in their lives (both professionally and personally), what obstacles to writing teachers may face, and how writing groups may offer support and help teachers work beyond these challenges.

WRITING AS INVENTION

Considering teacher-writers through the lens of *invention* helps highlight their professional and personal knowledge and creativity, drawing attention to the multiple things they may invent: texts, writing practices, writing communities, and even identities as writers. But what can it mean to be a teacher-writer (or even just a writer)? What do writers *do*, and how can foregrounding creativity help us make sense of those writing practices?

Writing represents an active process. This book explores the practices and processes teacher-writers engage in as they write, thereby emphasizing the many things teacher-writers are *doing* as they compose and the significance of these actions in their personal and professional lives. Paul Prior (2004) explains:

> Writing moves forward (and backward) in fits and starts, with pauses and flurries, discontinuities and conflicts. Situated acts of *composing/inscription* are themselves complex composites. Writers are not only *inscribing text*. They are also repeatedly *rereading* text that they've written, *revising* text as they write as well, going back later to revise, pausing to *read other texts* (their own notes, texts they have written, source materials, inspirations), pausing to *think and plan*. (p. 172, italics in original)

Here, Prior highlights the multiple layers and opportunities for invention associated with writing. Rather than portraying writing as a linear process that marches neatly from brainstorming to drafting to revising, Prior reminds us of the recursive nature of writing and the overlapping actions writers take. When we write, we also read and think and plan, moving back and forth across our text. These writing practices are inherently creative in nature, as we invent new text, reenvision what we have already written, and imagine possibilities and next steps.

Writing practices are also inherently social, not only as a writer composes a text, but also as a writer imagines that text being read by other people. Too often, writing is portrayed as a solitary act, conjuring images of a lone individual bent over a computer keyboard or notebook. It may be hard to get excited about that kind of writing, especially after a long day of teaching! Yet from a rhetorical standpoint, invention itself is a social process. As rhetorician Karen LeFevre explains in *Invention As a Social Act* (1987), rhetorical invention is "initiated by writers and completed by readers" and extends "over time through a series of transactions and texts" (p. 1). When we begin to imagine an audience reading our writing, we enter into conversation with that audience, predicting and wondering about how they may interpret our written words.

Sometimes this audience awareness can cause anxiety or uncertainty, which is when having a group of trusted writer friends can be particularly useful. A writing group can provide members with a safe and productive first audience, where authors might seek varied feedback and refine their approaches to a text. LeFevre notes that "invention becomes explicitly social when writers involve other people as collaborators, or as reviewers whose comments aid invention, or as 'resonators' who nourish the development of ideas" (p. 2). This description is an accurate portrayal of what happens in the writing group meetings featured in this book, where teacher-writers collaborate to brainstorm ideas, review texts-in-progress, and discuss ideas and writing decisions.

Throughout our writing group experiences, *talk* features prominently in our social, inventive processes. Prior (2004) explains that following a writer's process involves, among other things, "tracing exchanges (spoken or written) between people, exchanges in which the content and purposes of a text may be imagined and planned, in which specific language may even be 'drafted' out in talk" (pp. 167–168). The teacher-writers featured in this book talk a great deal about writing, and these spoken exchanges both reveal and shape the composition of a text. As future chapters will demonstrate, talk can help writers reshape content, genre, organization, and even purpose of a text, and writers often orally rehearse language they might later incorporate into revisions.

When we think of writing as social and creative in these ways, the significance of teacher-writers' experiences while writing also becomes apparent. It can be tempting to think about the purpose and outcomes of teachers' writing in reductive ways, focusing narrowly on the production of texts. Yet much happens across a writer's creative processes, and these experiences are important in themselves. Bob Yagelski (2009) observes that focusing only on the textual products of writing "tends to neglect the effect of the *act of writing* on the writer's sense of being in the moment and over time. Whatever happens to a text *after* it is written does not affect what is happening to (or *in*) the writer *as she or he is writing that text*" (p. 17, italics in original). To illustrate this concept, Yagelski describes an essay a student wrote about her mother, which he observed was "about making sense of a crucial experience that continues to shape her life . . . about *being* in a challenging world." In this example, he notes that the actual written text may be "irrelevant in view of what the experience of writing it might have meant to her" (p. 19). This emphasis on experience aligns with what Karen said she was seeking in a writing group in the first place. She did not reference wanting simply to compose several powerful texts; rather, she said she wanted opportunities to develop relationships and try out writing for herself.

In her study of participants from a National Writing Project (NWP) summer institute, Anne Elrod Whitney (2008) observed that many participants described their experience as "transformative," crediting the writing they did and the support they experienced as particularly significant. Writing about his own experience in an NWP summer institute, teacher David Grosskopf (2004) described the way the act of writing helped him feel "fully awake" and "most alive." He explained, "It's not merely the production of writing—even good writing, and the satisfaction that brings—that has powered my sense of vitality; it is the act of writing itself."

Both Grosskopf and Yagelski highlight the ways that, through acts of composing text, writers may experience and compose ways of being in the world. Indeed, Grosskopf draws a parallel between "composing a poem and composing a life." Thus, as teacher-writers invent text, they are also, in a way, inventing and *being invented*, by themselves and others, within the social context of writing group meetings. Rhetorician Debra Hawhee (2002) notes that in these experiences "one invents and is invented, one writes and is written" (pp. 17–18), highlighting the ways inventive acts may shape texts as well as the writers and their future creative acts.

This book seeks to help teacher-writers think expansively about writing practices, purposes for writing, and what may be invented in the process. As teacher-writers, while we may write to compose texts, and those texts may be significant outcomes of our efforts, sometimes our experiences *while* writing may carry even more significance. And those experiences may have particular impact and worth when they are shared with other writers, within the social context of a writing group. As we compose together and share our thinking, we create not only texts but also new ways of *doing* writing. We compose ways of being writers, ways of playing with language, and ways of finding joy in composing texts.

WHY WRITE? BENEFITS FOR TEACHER-WRITERS

During the same meeting that opens this chapter, Karen also reflects on how her writing experiences changed over the course of our first year together. She recalls, "In the beginning of our writing group I wrote mostly about classroom experiences. But it was like writing to *sort through* what was happening. And it was nice . . . and I *know* I wouldn't have written if I wasn't in this group. For sure." Several of us quickly agree, our voices overlapping across our online call. "I would've just come home and had a bottle of wine," Karen adds, laughing, and I quickly join in. "But instead, I came home and had a bottle of wine *and wrote*, and I think it was more healthy."

Now we are all laughing, and Karen has to wait a moment before she can continue. "But then I also shifted and I was like, 'Well, I still should be writing cause I'm in a writing group, but I'm sick of thinking about school.' And I, you know, started to write about . . . my study abroad trip. Things like that. And I think . . . I wouldn't have written that either. It was also a nice chance to shift and think about myself as a writer, but to also think about myself as like, you know, a more complicated human being than just a teacher. That helped me do that."

I think about Karen's comments, as well as the many experiences I have shared with her and the other three members of our writing group, when people ask about the benefits associated with teacher-writers and writing groups. Karen's comments highlight the way a writing group can provide an incentive and audience for a teacher's writing. She also notes some of the varied purposes for her writing: to sort through her teaching experiences and to explore topics that have significance in her life. Her writing experiences allow her to make sense of an intense first year of teaching, and also to remind herself that "teacher" is just one part of her full and "more complicated" identity.

Too often, our writing is presented as primarily in service to our profession or our students, with teachers encouraged to write in order to unlock greater pedagogical opportunities and understandings. These are tremendously worthy reasons for us to write. But Karen's comments, and the coming chapters of this book, highlight additional and more personal significance of our social, creative acts of writing. We write to have fun, to interact with each other, and to explore. We write to experience our lives in different ways, to work through ideas, and to play with language. We often are laughing as we talk together, and there is, indeed, something healthy about that.

Pedagogical Opportunities

Regardless of whether it is our primary goal, our writing does create significant opportunities for our teaching. There is a great deal of evidence that teachers' writing practices may inform and enhance their writing pedagogies, allowing them to develop writing and teaching strategies, abilities to empathize with student writers, and valuable understandings about writing (Atwell, 1998; Calkins, 1986; Dahl, 1992; Gillespie, 1985; Kittle, 2008; Murray, 1968). In her book *Write Beside Them*, experienced English teacher and literacy coach Penny Kittle (2008) describes teachers' writing practices as "essential" to their work as writing teachers (p. 8). Kittle explains that teacher-writers have the ability to use their own writing to show or demonstrate for students how to write, to literally "write beside them," rather than merely telling students what to do. In fact, she tells teachers, "You are the most important writer in the room" (p. 8). Kittle also points to writing as a key part of what feeds her and makes her love teaching.

As teacher-writers, we gain access to examples from our own writing lives that we may use to illustrate concepts and strategies for students. Rather than having to rely on models only from students or professional writers, we also can use our own experiences to show strategies for overcoming a writing hurdle, experimenting with different techniques, or revising our writing (Perry, 1995; Ray & Laminack, 2001). Teacher Tim Gillespie (1991) observes that when we model writing strategies in this way, we draw upon techniques familiar to violin teachers, shop teachers, and pottery teachers, who demonstrate for students how to hold an instrument, work a tool, or shape a clay pot. "When we writing teachers write and share our work with students," Gillespie says, "we are asserting ourselves as equally professional" (p. 6). Writing teacher Rosemary Perry (1995) agrees, claiming that modeling is one of the most effective methods she has found for teaching the writing process and for demonstrating the ways she uses writing in her life outside teaching.

Jillian, another member of the writing group featured in this book, echoes these sentiments, proclaiming that as teacher-writers, "We're buying what we're selling!" She adds, "When you are teaching about writing, if it's not something that you do in your everyday life," then it can seem "like [you are saying] the purpose of writing is to get a good grade in school." But as a teacher-writer, she says she can use her own writing life to highlight the significance of writing beyond grades and school, "because *we* have this experience where writing really was—*is*—important to us, and we are able to express ourselves in writing." Jillian finds power in being "able to share that with our students . . . that we are *still growing* as writers and we are still carving out that time."

As teacher-writers, we also may find ourselves able to respond to student-writers with greater empathy, positioning ourselves as members of our classroom writing communities. When we have our own experiences with writing, and perhaps especially when those experiences include struggle and uncertainty, we may better understand what it feels like for our students to work with unfamiliar genres or feel uncomfortable sharing their writing with others. Discussing our writing difficulties with student writers can help them see that even teachers experience frustration as we struggle to use written language to express meaning. Engaging in our own writing, therefore, helps "expand our repertoire of useful responses to students" (Gillespie, 1991, p. 5).

When we engage in and reflect on our own writing projects, we have the potential to develop insights and opportunities for our teaching that may be otherwise unavailable to us. Yet translating our own writing experiences into classroom practice is not necessarily automatic. Students benefit most when teachers also inquire into their own writing experiences and strategies, explore connections with their teaching, and endeavor to make some of their practices public within their classroom communities. Sheridan Blau (1999) describes the significance of this inquiry within the National Writing Project, where "teachers examine the writing process and the perils and challenges of writing from the inside, with themselves as experimental subjects, interrogating in the experiment their own assumptions about writing and learning to write, and exploring the most useful ways to respond to writing." This deeply reflective work is inherently social in nature, and a teacher writing group may offer important support for this collaborative inquiry into writing practices and teaching.

Enhanced Participation in the Field

Teachers also are encouraged to write about (and even publish) their teaching practices to reflect on and share knowledge with other professionals. Within the context of the National Writing Project, Sheridan Blau (1999) discusses the ways that teachers' writing may help them "clarify and articulate their instructional goals both to themselves and to their colleagues," enabling them to become "principal contributors to the professional learning of their colleagues." Similarly, author Vivian Gussin Paley (1989) notes that her practice of writing down what happened in her class played a critical role in making sense of and learning from those experiences. Again, writing groups are well-positioned to support teachers' collaborative inquiry into practice, as they use writing to explore teaching and engage in focused reflection (Robbins et al., 2006).

Additionally, the social practices of writing groups may help participants make the first moves toward sharing teaching practices (and writing) more publicly. In an article in the NWP publication *The Quarterly*, Grace McEntee (1998) notes how commonly schools and teaching are studied from the outside, whereas teachers are uniquely suited to write from within the knowledge and context of schooling. Says McEntee, writing about practice allows teachers to "see students, colleagues, parents, the school in new ways," with writing groups serving as "vehicles for probing more deeply" (p. 21).

Research has shown that teachers who publish in professional practitioner journals report an increased sense of authority related to the content or pedagogical practices they wrote about (Whitney et al., 2012). These findings highlight the potential for teacher-writers to claim a sense of authority in shaping what is known about writing instruction, rather than being positioned primarily as recipients or consumers of other people's knowledge.

AND YET . . . CHALLENGES FOR TEACHER-WRITERS

Clearly, there are a host of personal and professional benefits that may open up to teacher-writers. Yet writing and making one's writing public, whether in the classroom or more broadly with other teachers, can easily feel like one more thing added onto an already full professional to-do list. It can be easy to feel intimidated by these ideas and experience obstacles to pursuing writing, ranging from limited time and support to narrow notions of what "counts" as writing. In the early 1990s, in a heated essay published in the National Council of Teachers of English publication *English Journal*, high school English teacher Karen Jost became a voice for teachers frustrated by messages that they should add writing to all the other work they do for their jobs. Jost (1990) took the controversial stand that *"high-school writing teachers should not write"* (pp. 65, italics in original), stating that they do not have teaching loads or school support to engage in "serious writing," and that she was tired of feeling guilty for not doing so.

Jost's (1990) essay, while written some time ago, still calls attention to constraints teachers may face when they pursue their own writing projects, including different understandings of what being a "teacher-writer" entails. However well-intentioned the messages may be, Jost points out that encouragement for teachers to write can easily be experienced as a "dictum" or a guilt trip, implying that writing is a part of being a "good" teacher and seeming to pass judgment on those who choose not to pursue it. As Jost observes, teachers often are overwhelmed with professional obligations, may not have much support within a school community, and simply may not have time to do anything else in service of their profession.

Schools often do not have existing ways to support communities of teacher-writers (Blau, 1999), leading many teachers to seek support in external contexts, such as the National Writing Project. Yet even after a powerful experience writing in an NWP summer institute, many teachers return to school and find their "confidence and idealism are tested by staggering class loads, and their reflective thinking is shattered by committee meetings, attendance lists, and hall duty," leading many teacher-writers to become "former writers as the school year progresses" (Gere, 1980, p. 2). In today's teaching contexts that include high-stakes teacher evaluations, standardized curricula, and student testing, it is all the more evident that the demands associated with teaching are not trivial.

Jost's (1990) essay also highlights another issue that can dissuade teachers from writing: narrow concepts of what really "counts" as writing. Jost articulates a belief that teacher-writers must engage in "serious writing," perhaps akin to what a professional novelist or poet might do in writing literary works for publication. It is no wonder that this concept of writing would present a significant obstacle for many teachers. Yet this notion of writing discounts the many dabbling, exploratory, and reflective efforts that teacher-writers often describe as the most satisfying. Karen's writing about her classroom and study abroad experiences likely would not fall within this narrow construct of "serious writing," and yet Karen clearly noted the significance these texts held for her. This book explicitly seeks to expand notions of what teachers' writing may look like, deliberately making space for a variety of texts, genres, and experiences as writers.

Jost's (1990) essay spurred a deluge of responses, with the *English Journal* receiving more reader letters in 2 weeks than they usually received over 7 months (Nelms, 1990). Clearly, the topic had struck a nerve. Read together, these various essays and letters echo the benefits and challenges associated with teacher writing outlined in this chapter. Weighing all of these together, however, I have to agree with Tim Gillespie's (1995) assessment: "Is the investment of time in writing worth the return for us as time-pressed teachers? I still have to say, emphatically, yes. If and when we can manage it, writing offers us many benefits" (p. 41).

SUPPORT STRUCTURES: TEACHER WRITING GROUPS

The importance of social support for writing is a common theme among teacher-writers, with many noting the critical necessity of having a community within which to share writing (Bridgford, 2001; Hicks et al., 2013; Rosenthal, 2003; Simone, 1995). Writing groups can provide a great source of this support. In reflecting on his participation in an NWP summer institute, teacher Robert Burroughs (1995) observed, "Writing groups may well be the most memorable experience," providing teachers a means to get help with writing across different stages (p. 3). Burroughs noted that his NWP writing group supported him by encouraging and validating him at the early stages of a piece of writing, then helping him shape a piece as it developed, and ultimately offering reactions (and likely additional validation) with the finished piece.

Other teacher-writers also describe the way participation in a writing group can provide a sense of audience, accountability, incentive, and support, helping them pursue their own writing projects (Durst, 1992; Elrod, 2003; Flythe, 1989; Hicks et al., 2013; Morris & Haight, 1993; Robbins et al., 2006; Williams, 1990). Ann Dobie (2008), a National Writing Project site director, notes that writing groups can provide "encouragement to keep going, learning from each other, and deepening connections with one another and with one's writing." For these reasons, she encourages teachers completing an NWP summer institute to form or continue writing groups once they return to school, in order to extend support into the school year.

As noted above, writing groups can help teachers explore their actual writing practices, calling attention to what they *do* as writers. Participation in a writing group also may position teachers to reflect on and, if they choose, use writing to inform and share teaching practices. For example, writing group discussions can remind teachers of what it is like to be student writers, showing the complexities of revision and responding to writing (Durst, 1992; Williams, 1990). By discussing their experiences seeking and using feedback with other writers, teachers may uncover opportunities worth sharing in their own classrooms.

Writing groups like the one featured in this book offer a rich context for teachers to explore and invent writing practices, laying the groundwork for enjoyment and mutual support. Most importantly, writing groups may offer the necessary support to help teachers overcome constraints they may face as writers, including limited time and ways of thinking about writing. Because it still can be a challenge for writing groups to find time to meet, especially when members are geographically dispersed, online writing groups may offer a particularly attractive option.

THE TEACHER-WRITER: THE CHAPTERS TO COME

The following chapters focus on an online teacher writing group during our first year of writing together. This is a writing group comprised of five teachers, teaching in a variety of contexts, and spread across several states. We meet almost exclusively online. As I share the talk, texts, writing practices, and ways of being teacher-writers that we create across that first year as a writing group, I hope other teachers may see opportunities to pursue their own writing.

One of the goals of this book is to help teachers imagine ways to pursue meaningful writing, both for personal and professional purposes. In doing so, this book continually situates writing as a creative, social process, foregrounding what teacher-writers are *doing* in talk and writing as they compose texts. Echoing Karen's observation that her writing allows her to focus energy on her interests both within and beyond the classroom, the coming chapters foreground teachers as whole people whose experiences as writers matter regardless of the particular texts, teaching strategies, and professional work they may invent.

There are many ways teachers may enter and sustain writing projects. Chapter 2 introduces the online teacher writing group featured throughout the rest of the book, elaborating on our shared commitments, logistics for meeting online, and regular routines. Chapters 3 through 7 then offer portraits of teacher-writers in action, sharing talk and texts from our first year of writing group meetings. Chapter 3 invites readers into an online meeting from start to finish, to illustrate how meetings unfold and to demonstrate ways teacher-writers may create time and opportunities for writing. Then Chapter 4 highlights strategies teachers may use to find writing opportunities in everyday places and to sustain energy for some texts across time. Chapter 5 presents ways teachers may reclaim professional and academic writing projects to create cohesion across their writing lives. Chapters 6 and 7 then examine ways that teacher-writers may use writing and writing group practices to compose ways of being and ways of interacting with others. Looking across and beyond the full first year of our writing, Chapter 8 connects the themes and strategies across the preceding chapters.

Overall, this book seeks to foster inquiry: What happens when we reposition writing in teachers' lives and foreground creativity and play? What happens when we engage in writing as a social and interactive endeavor? What might we gain when we focus less on how to "be a writer" and instead consider how we might purposefully "do writing"—in whatever ways it works in our lives? For the writing group members featured in this book, it is in the social practices associated with writing that we find the most significant benefits.

Teachers' Writing: Understandings and Opportunities

Expanding Concepts of Writing

- Writing is recursive in nature. Rather than following a linear process, most writers move back and forth across a text, reenvisioning what they have already written and imagining next steps. When they write, they also read and think and plan.
- Writing has an inherently social element. A text may be written by an author, but it is often interpreted and experienced by a reader. When a writer envisions a reader's reaction, the writer anticipates a social interaction. Similarly, when a writer brings a text to other writers for feedback, the interaction that ensues is also social in nature.
- Talk can be a critical part of a writer's processes. Through talking with others, a writer may gain support reshaping the content, genre, organization, and even purpose of a text. Many writers also find it useful to orally rehearse language for later revisions.
- A writer's experiences while writing are significant in themselves. Regardless of what happens to a given text, the act of writing can be transformative.

Benefits for Teacher-Writers

- Teacher-writers gain access to examples from their own writing lives, which they may use to illustrate concepts and strategies for students. Through their own writing, teacher-writers also may be able to respond to student-writers with greater empathy, positioning themselves as members of their classroom writing community.
- Writing is a useful means of inquiry, through which teachers may explore and reflect on teaching practices.
- When teachers publish or share professional writing, they are able to participate in making and sharing knowledge in their profession. Teachers who publish in professional journals often report an increased sense of authority.

CHAPTER 2

A "Breathing Space"

Creating an Online Teacher Writing Group

What makes a fire burn
is space between the logs,
a breathing space.
Too much of a good thing,
too many logs
packed in too tight
can douse the flames
almost as surely
as a pail of water would. . . .
So building fires
requires attention
to the spaces in between,
as much as to the wood.

—Judy Brown, "Fire" (2006)

I love this poem, because it captures a truly familiar feeling: the urge to add just a little bit more into an already busy life, whether out of a sense of interest or duty. One more well-intentioned log, to better my classroom or my students' experiences. Judy Brown's words serve as a reminder, however, of the significance of *space* in allowing a fire to truly burn.

I felt the need for this space acutely in my life when I reached out to begin this writing group. I was balancing my doctoral studies with teaching in an education program at a large university. I had a daughter and family at home, over an hour away from campus. My life seemed to revolve around teaching, parenting, and my own graduate studies. I missed writing for myself, playing with language, and talking about creativity and craft. I also was aware of how much my writing life did relate to my teaching life, but I did not feel like I had time to add more work or obligations to my schedule. I wondered how I could create space to write and talk with other writers.

This chapter shares the way our writing group began, as well as the decisions and commitments we made to create space for sustainable writing practices in our lives. It also introduces each member of the writing group, providing a glimpse into the people behind the conversations and written texts that fill the coming chapters. I hope this chapter may be useful for other teacher writing groups, as you strive to articulate goals and agreements, identify useful technology to support online or in-person writing groups, and plan routines for meetings.

INTRODUCTION TO OUR WRITING GROUP

I first met my fellow writing group members when they were preservice teachers in a series of curriculum and literacy teaching methods courses I taught at the university. Because I care about helping teachers develop and share writing practices, I incorporated lots of writing into my teaching. We wrote and provided feedback on each other's poetry, lesson plans, essays, inquiries into teaching, and reflections on our experiences. We read mentor texts and discussed the relationship between a writer's purpose, craft decisions, and effect on readers. We analyzed each of these experiences, the strategies we used and developed, and the role of talk and inquiry. On many occasions I wrote alongside my students, sharing a rough draft of a poem to model the power of early feedback, opening up my own lesson plans and reflections as illustrative examples, and sharing pages from my writing notebooks to demonstrate the way ideas develop over time.

After spending four semesters together as a cohort, my students were preparing for graduation and their first teaching jobs. The campus grounds were just starting to come back to life after a long, gray Midwestern winter; the sun was shining again and new growth rustled in the spring breezes. As my students prepared to take teaching jobs across the country, I wondered what would happen to the writing practices we had shared. I was aware of how easily the time demands of first-year teaching could overwhelm teachers' own writing. I, too, sought to balance my teaching and writing amid my professional and family life.

Thus, wanting to create space in my own life for writing and wanting to support my soon-to-be-former students in doing the same, I pitched the idea of starting a writing group. I asked if anyone would be interested in continuing to write together after graduation. It would be a writing group where we could pursue our own writing projects and interests, and I would be a fellow member in the group, no longer their instructor. I was delighted when four women responded to my invitation: Karen, Jillian, Christina, and Nell. [Note: With the exception of Jillian and Christina, who have elected to use their own names, all other names used throughout this text are pseudonyms. Additionally, other identifying features have either been removed, modified, or given pseudonyms as well.]

Five writers felt like a good number to start with: enough people to have a discussion, but not too many to prevent us each from sharing writing at every meeting. We made only the most general of plans that spring, deciding to begin meeting in the fall, after they started in their new jobs. Over the summer we stayed in touch via email, sharing our unfolding teaching plans and a little bit of what we each hoped to get out of a writing group.

As I write this book, our group has been meeting together for over 8 years, and much has changed in each of our lives. Because this book focuses on our first year together as a writing group, highlighting our practices as an emerging cohort, I introduce each member based on her circumstances at that time in our lives.

Karen

As Karen tells us in Chapter 1, "The main reason I joined, to be honest, was because I wanted to talk with you all." After spending almost two years together with other members of her university cohort, Karen moved out of state, several hundred miles from home, to accept her first teaching job. Her early weeks in her new home were consumed not only with establishing her classroom, but also with the complexities of laying down roots and creating a sense of home. She tells us, "I love the city, but it's also sort of weird being here without family. I am meeting friends in the neighborhood and the staff at my school is awesome :)." Karen also says she looks forward to writing for *herself*, beyond academic or professional writing, and she emails us one day early in the year with the joking command, "If you are reading this right now, you should text me at some point to say 'Write Karen!'"

Outgoing, spontaneous, and funny, Karen has what one group member describes as "infectious laughter" and a "hilarious, unexpected, passionate" personality. An engaging storyteller, Karen often shares tales about her classroom and life, and she easily reduces the rest of us to laughter. Her stories are peppered with jokes, vocal impressions of friends and students, and emotional honesty. She does not shrink from writing or saying what she feels, and her openness often creates space for the rest of us to do the same. Karen's first teaching job, in an urban 8th-grade classroom, is challenging in many ways, especially as Karen seeks to create a respectful classroom climate amid considerable schoolwide instability. Her ultimate success in this teaching situation is a testament to her determination and resilience, which are fueled by her quick sense of humor and deep care for her students.

Jillian

Jillian also says she joined the writing group largely because she wanted to stay in touch with us as she left the university and entered her first teaching job. Married with two sons, Jillian is able to find a job teaching 6th-grade English Language Arts in a suburban elementary school not too far from her home. She also coaches a running program for elementary girls. Easygoing, honest, and open, Jillian cares deeply for her family, friends, and students.

Jillian's two young sons are often present in our writing group meetings, whether through her writing or as their small voices spill into our online conversations. We can easily picture Jacob's floppy blonde hair and Bryan's "toothy grin" and "crinkly diaper butt" as we hear them ask for a snack or argue over a game in the background. Jillian's oldest son is the same age as my daughter, and we have fun sharing stories of our adventures in parenthood, from potty-training escapades and daycare dilemmas to birthday party planning.

As one group member says, Jillian is "warm, patient, creative," somehow able to multitask between preparing dinner, interacting with her husband and sons, and offering thoughtful feedback on a fellow group member's writing. Speaking slowly and deliberately at times, Jillian thinks deeply about her writing and her responses to others. She is also quick to add a note of levity to our conversations, laughing over an experience in her classroom or with her boys. She is always ready to commiserate or empathize with other members of the group. As a writing group member, Jillian says she hopes to have fun with us, to explore her personal writing, and to "enjoy writing again."

Christina

Like Jillian, Christina is married, and her first teaching job is in a city relatively close to her home, allowing her to avoid moving. As we form our writing group, Christina describes wanting to give herself "permission to make personal writing a priority in the midst of a busy schedule filled with other very important priorities." Not only does Christina teach English as a Second Language at the middle and high school levels, but she is also the ESL coordinator for the whole district. Her school is an urban charter school that had not met AYP (Adequate Yearly Progress), raising the concern that her job may not be completely secure if improvements are not made. But Christina says she loves "being able to work with students at all of the grade levels," enjoying the way the younger and older students have different energy levels and interests. Christina also works several evenings a week at a local restaurant, a job she has held since college. Her first year of teaching draws on Christina's strengths: her flexibility, efficiency, organization, and ability to juggle demanding situations.

Even as an undergraduate, Christina had a strong professional presence as a teacher. She spoke with quiet authority in discussions, able to reframe and synthesize diverse perspectives. Her teaching job and busy schedule place intense demands on her, and Christina often turns to writing to help her articulate and work through these challenges, saying she wants "to examine and make sense out of my memories and experiences." Not surprisingly, another group member describes Christina as "always learning" and "an expert in so much," portraying Christina's voice in our group meetings as "smooth and sure and always questioning." Christina is generous with her time and thoughtful feedback, and she is knowledgeable about technology. While she is sometimes more reserved than other group members during our first year together, perhaps less apt to crack a joke, Christina is quick to laugh in response to someone else's antics.

Nell

For Nell, who took a teaching job some distance from home like Karen, the autumn brings both a new job and a new home. After our first writing group meeting, Nell reflects on "how nice it is to talk to people that I've known for a few years," articulating a sentiment that often is echoed by other group members. Nell teaches English as a Second Language in a private boarding school, so she has a slightly unusual schedule, often teaching on Saturdays or offering evening tutorials for her students. Her new home is in a rural area, and she tells us, "Squirrels keep nibbling at the jack-o-lanterns I have on my front stoop. I've trapped and killed my seventh mouse recently, and I keep finding bees crawling around in my carpet, getting caught in my lamps, or stinging me in the foot in my bathroom."

When it comes to writing, Nell says, "I'd like to make writing an integral part of my life, like working or flossing. I'd like to experiment with different genres, especially humor writing!" With a wry sense of humor that often causes our group to dissolve into laughter, Nell is, as a fellow group member describes her, a true "Renaissance woman." Indeed, there are many sides to Nell, including her love for Harry Potter, her musical talent (she plays trombone in a local community college band), and her enjoyment of both camping and the arts. Introspective and thoughtful, Nell often uses writing to ponder her relationships, her life, and her students' lives, leading another group member to describe her as "brave in her writing," and observe that Nell "explores a variety of experiences, emotions, and genres." Nell is curious and open to feedback, and her playful sense of humor always keep meetings lively and fun.

Christine (me)

I am the fifth member of the writing group. I tell Karen, Jillian, Christina, and Nell that I want "to carve out more time to write for my own purposes . . . to use writing to help me cherish some of my experiences and to help me process and make sense of others." Not unlike other teachers, I write all the time, but I yearn for more play and creative outlets. I hope for inspiration and incentive and support as a writer. I also had grown close to the other writing group members and am eager to stay in touch with them after they graduate.

After teaching middle school and high school English for 10 years, as we start our writing group I am immersed in my doctoral program and teach preservice language arts teachers at the university level. I live with my daughter, husband, and two aged Labrador Retrievers, over an hour from campus, so I spend some full days on campus and others working from home. Prior to pursuing my doctorate and teaching university classes, I had worked in rural, urban, and suburban districts, and I had been a secondary English department coordinator, mentor teacher, and literacy coach. While teaching high school I had sought out writing retreats and workshops for myself, and I am craving the opportunity to write for myself again.

My Roles in the Writing Group

My roles in our group are multilayered. Most important, I am a fellow writer, seeking to develop a writing life while teaching, just as the other members are. Because I had been the other members' university instructor, I knew that we would all need to transition from teacher-student to writer-writer relationships. I also have an interest in studying and learning from our writing group. For me, navigating these roles involves consistently foregrounding my role as a writer, while also being open and explicit and flexible.

As a fellow writer, I share my texts and experiment with writing strategies alongside other group members. I write things I would not have written, in ways I would not have written them, were it not for the conversations and support of my fellow group members. Therefore, my inquiry into this project has never been that of an outside observer, watching what *they* did. My inquiry is into what *we* invent, in various ways and across months of meetings and texts and conversations.

During this first year as a writing group, sometimes I intentionally modeled options for what we might share, as a way of making "space" for additional opportunities. I deliberately shared personal writing from the start, such as poems about family and about my love for young adult fantasy novels. I genuinely wanted feedback to help me develop these pieces, and I also wanted my group members to get to know other sides of me, beyond what may have come up in our university classroom. Because I believe in sharing writing even at early stages, I purposefully brought some writing when it was still unformed, and I often asked group members if they had ideas they wanted to discuss for future writing. I also sometimes shared different genres of writing, such as when I brought an essay on my teaching and a letter to a friend. These were purposeful moves on my part, bringing texts that I wanted to improve while intentionally modeling different possibilities for what we could share in group meetings. After I shared my letter and essay, I noticed other members began sharing pieces they were writing for outside audiences as well.

At our first meeting, when I introduced the possibility of studying our group, I emphasized that the group would be formed and would meet regardless of whether or not I studied it. I told other group members that they could choose to be identified by pseudonyms, and I emphasized that they had the final say on what texts or talk I collected and included in my study. For the same reason, I chose to delay audiotaping our meetings until our group had been meeting for 3 months and we were more comfortable together. Thus, while we certainly talked about the fact that I was studying our writing group, and while my research came up sometimes in the context of our conversations about writing, I participated in the group primarily as a fellow writer.

In studying our writing group, I took an ethnographic approach for gathering the talk and texts associated with 13 months of writing group meetings. I wrote fieldnotes, audiorecorded and transcribed group meetings, gathered shared texts, annotated and coded my data, and wrote countless analytical and theoretical memos (Bogdan & Biklen, 2007; Emerson, Fretz, & Shaw, 1995; Heath & Street, 2008). These varied texts and data provide the examples of the writing group conversations shared throughout the rest of the book. (A list of all the writings shared in our first year can be found in Appendix A, and more information on my research approaches can be found in Appendix B).

CENTRAL COMMITMENTS IN DEVELOPING OUR WRITING GROUP

When I first pitched the idea of a writing group, I envisioned a group like some I had read or heard about, perhaps meeting at a corner table in a coffee shop, where we might share food, discuss writing, and catch up with each other. This vision quickly changed, however, when Nell and Karen accepted teaching jobs far from campus. If we all wanted to participate, our meetings would have to move online. This decision turned out to be fortuitous for me as well; within our first year writing together, I also moved out of state.

Before we could contemplate specific logistics regarding *how* to create our online writing group experience, we had to consider what we wanted that experience to entail. What did each of us want to get out of the writing group? We started with the knowledge that we were all busy, with many competing demands for our time and energy. We faced a challenge: How could we prevent our writing endeavors from feeling like well-intentioned "logs" that may actually smother our "fires"? How could we instead create a generative space for writing?

As we began meeting, we explored these challenges, and our early discussions helped us voice goals and commitments. This process was, as noted in Chapter 1, a deeply social and creative endeavor. We talked about wanting a reason to write, feedback on our writing, a means to get more comfortable (and feel more authentic) teaching writing to students, and a way to keep in touch with each other. We talked about wanting our writing group to be fun and relaxed, a way to help us make writing a part of our lives.

Some of the most important work we did in early meetings involved defining our shared commitments, which then framed our meetings and served as the foundation for our creative work as writers.

First, we all wanted to *develop our relationships with each other*. As we scattered into new jobs and, in some cases, hometowns, our writing group provided an opportunity to gather and talk with trusted friends. Prioritizing personal relationships also provides an added incentive to come to group meetings, especially after a long day of teaching, and these relationships help us feel comfortable sharing personal writing with each other. It takes courage and trust to share writing, even when that writing is not particularly personal in nature (Dawson, 2009; Gillespie, 1991). For this to happen, we prioritize building time into our meetings just to talk, to continue to get to know each other and develop the relationships that will support us as we share our writing.

We also wanted to *create opportunities to pursue writing that we initiate*. While all five of us write daily as a part of work and school, we do not choose the vast majority of what we write based on our own enjoyment or creative purposes. In this writing group, we wanted to explore writing that we initiated, which Janet Emig calls "self-sponsored writing" (Emig, 1971), where we could experiment with genre, topic, style, and technique. We hoped that the support and interaction from group members would help us explore possibilities as writers and create texts that were personally meaningful to us.

To avoid having our writing group create a sense of additional stress or obligation, we talked about ways to *keep the group flexible and responsive* to our lives. We each want to make time to write, but no group member needs a source of stress or potential guilt. We each have moments where we have barely enough time to manage our professional and personal commitments. In those moments, we still want to feel welcome at writing group meetings, without any expectation to apologize for not bringing writing. We tried to be realistic as we decided how often to meet and what we would do in preparation for those meetings. From the beginning, we acknowledged that our group could change, depending on what worked for us, and we agreed to talk about how our experiences unfolded. Overall, we each want the group to be something we look forward to attending, and that vision requires us to be honest and open with each other about what we can do and how we want to participate.

Part of our commitment to flexibility involves agreeing that we each can *choose what writing to bring* (or whether to bring any writing at all) to each meeting. If we truly believe that feedback is useful across one's writing process, then we have to ensure that we can bring even the simplest beginning of a text. Choice is often emphasized in writing pedagogies, ranging from students having agency over what to write (Atwell, 1998; Fletcher, 1993) to students having flexibility in how to respond to an assignment (Hillocks,

1995; Smagorinsky, Johannessen, Kahn, & McCann, 2010). In our writing group, I hoped we also could consider our right to choose *how* to participate in meetings. Sharing ideas for future writing, and even just participating in conversations about other members' texts, have definite value. We make space for any type of writing at meetings, even if the text is not something we initiate (e.g., professional or academic writing), thereby allowing us to offer writing support across genres and contexts.

Each of the above decisions led to our final commitment: *our writing group meetings are live and talk-based.* Building talk about writing had been a focus of my instruction throughout the methods courses I had taught, and I believe in the importance of oral conversations in helping an author develop ideas, clarify purpose and desired effect, and make sense of writing choices and possibilities for revision (Dawson, 2009; Prior, 2004). In order to be able to have dialogue about our writing vision and goals, continue to develop our relationships with each other, and deeply explore even raw and unformed texts, we needed to be able to *talk* to each other during meetings. Being able to talk about our writing also allows us to foreground our experiences as we write, as well as explore ways of being writers and writing group members.

GETTING STARTED: CREATING OUR ONLINE WRITING GROUP

Articulating our shared commitments to talk-based meetings, in which we invest in our relationships with each other, prioritize writing we initiate, maintain flexibility and responsiveness to our needs, and choose what writing we share and how we participate, enabled us to then plan the logistics for our writing group meetings. We experimented with online technologies, especially audio/video conferencing and a private wiki, which formed the basis for our meeting experiences. We developed a schedule and routines, and we explored our own roles in writing group meetings.

Talking About Writing Online: Audio/Video Conferencing

Our first task was to figure out a way to talk about writing online. For writing groups that want to focus more specifically on textual production, this step may not be as necessary. There are models of writing groups where members share texts electronically and then provide written feedback to each other (Elrod, 2003; Rosenthal, 2003). These text-focused groups may be appealing for writers who seek regular, written feedback on their writing and also for writing groups that struggle to find a common meeting time. For our own group, with our commitment to being able to talk about our writing practices in addition to our texts, and with our interest in building relationships and multiple ways of participating, we needed live, talk-based meetings.

We decided to use Skype, a free, online phone program, as a means to hold five-way conference calls, using our computer microphones and speakers. In preparation for our first meeting, I emailed group members directions for downloading Skype and suggestions for getting started. We soon realized the value of getting online a few minutes early, to test sound and Internet connections. We also found it useful for each member to use earbuds, which helped eliminate feedback and background noise on our calls. Even so, we still had plenty of challenges in the first few months: We dropped calls, individuals got disconnected, and feedback sometimes interfered with our ability to hear each other. We tried to be creative when such problems occurred, and over time we got better and better at troubleshooting our technological problems. In the past several years Skype has improved their program significantly, so the frequency and resultant disruption of these issues has diminished.

When we first started meeting, Skype could not support a five-way video call, so we relied on audio for our conversations. Even today, if a group member does not have a strong Internet connection, the call may work better with just audio. We found that it is helpful if each group member creates a Skype profile with a good close-up picture; having these visual cues makes talking together seem more personal. We now use video conferencing regularly when we meet, which helps make our meetings feel even more natural. There are a number of options online groups can use for audio/video conferencing in addition to Skype, such as Google Hangout or FaceTime. Many of these options also include chat features, so group members can type a quick message if they have to step away from a call, experience technology issues, or want to share an online link.

In early meetings, when the online forum was most new, it took a little time to feel comfortable and natural with each other during meetings. It was harder to predict who would talk next, and it was easy to speak over each other. Our group soon developed oral cues to replace the visual ones we rely on during in-person interactions. As we gained experience in our online meetings, we also became less worried when we did cut each other off or speak at the same time; usually someone quickly defers ("you go ahead"), and the conversation picks right back up again. We also make a point of trying to set up face-to-face meetings on occasion, even just one a year, when we can gather in person. These in-person meetings are rare but welcome opportunities to reconnect.

Sharing Writing Online: A Private Wiki or Shared Cloud Storage

Being able to talk online in real time was just the first step; we also needed a way to share our writing with each other. To facilitate sharing a range of texts, some of which would be personal, I recommend establishing a secure, online space to organize writing and resources. Our group ruled out sharing texts via school email accounts, which are not private. We could have shared our writing each time via personal email, but it can get messy searching for the right email string during a meeting. Additionally, we found it useful to have all of our writing together, so we could easily reference past drafts or switch quickly between different writers' texts.

During our first several years, our group used a private wiki to meet these needs. A *wiki* is a collaborative website that can be edited (adding links and pages, uploading content) by any authorized user. For our writing group we created a private, password-protected space, giving only the five of us access to the wiki and to the writing posted there. The easiest way to create a wiki is by using a host site (called a "wiki farm"), which offers simple, step-by-step directions on how to build a wiki from scratch. We used Wikispaces, which is designed for education and academic contexts. To begin, each member created an account by going to the Wikispaces website (www.wikispaces.com). There are many online resources available to help you create a wiki, both on the wiki farm's website itself or by simply doing an online search for wiki tips. You also could achieve a similar effect by using an online cloud-based file sharing system, such as Dropbox or Google Drive.

For our group, we needed a simple organization scheme, which would help us each manage and share our own texts, keep our writing organized by date and author, and provide everyone access to shared files. To accomplish this, it is useful to think about how you want to access and use your online file storage. On the home page of our wiki, there is a link to a Shared Resources page, as well as links to a separate page for each of our members. On the Shared Resources page, we can each upload mentor texts, articles, links for other websites, or any resource we think may be useful for the group as a whole. Each of us then uses our individual wiki page to store our writing. Texts may be uploaded as files, which other members can download to read. Figure 2.1 illustrates this organizational structure.

It is easy enough to adapt this structure to Google Drive or Dropbox by simply using folders instead of the pages on a wiki: so, from a "home" folder, you would access additional folders for resources and member writing. Typically, if the "home" folder is shared with all members of the group, then anything created inside that home folder will also be shared. In recent years, our group has gravitated to using Google Drive to share files. Regardless of whether you use a wiki or Google Drive, once you have a basic organizational structure in place, you can adapt to suit your group members' needs and interests. For example, Christina decided she preferred using her blog to organize and share her writing, so she often shared a link to her blog with us. While Christina's blog is technically public, she can password-protect any entries she wants, sharing the password with us during writing group meetings.

Figure 2.1. Organization of Online Space for Sharing Writing

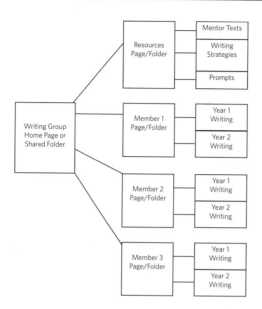

Scheduling Online Meetings

Once we settled on how to talk about and share our writing online, we decided on the timing and structure of our meetings. We needed to have enough time to write between meetings, and we needed to meet regularly enough to have some level of continuity. We gradually pieced together a plan to meet every other week. Group members were unanimous in choosing every other week, which Jillian explained, "Sounds like it'd give me enough time to write between meetings, so it wouldn't put added pressure on me, but also would be often enough to keep things moving along." Once that was decided, we set out to find a day and time that would work for our meetings, initially deciding to meet for 2 hours after school on alternate Thursday afternoons.

We have experimented with a number of different approaches to scheduling since then. We most commonly schedule our meetings using Google Calendar, to allow us each to confirm that we will be there and save the time in our schedules. When finding a common date and time is tricky, we sometimes turn to online polls (e.g., doodle.com or whenisgood.net), which help us propose multiple options efficiently. We have found the best method for scheduling to be either setting a permanent meeting time (e.g., every other week at a given day/time) or using the last few minutes of a meeting to set and confirm the next one.

Establishing Routines

In our first meeting, and over the first few months together, we ironed out some of the logistics for what we would do during and in preparation for our meetings. It took us several meetings to really get settled, as we refined goals for the rest of the semester and experimented with various online technologies. We considered whether we wanted to write together during meetings, perhaps in response to a shared invitational prompt, or bring our writing to meetings for discussion. We brainstormed what topics we might write about and explored ways to initiate our own projects. I invited group members to share strategies they had tried with their writing, and I introduced several writing exercises to help us get started (more details on these strategies are included in Chapter 4).

After those initial exploratory meetings, we started bringing writing to meetings and soon settled into a rhythm and a predictable structure. We begin meetings with what we call "reconnecting time" and then move into sharing our writing. Each person has an opportunity to share a text or idea for writing during each meeting, with time built in for response and feedback.

During our reconnecting time, we quite literally reconnect with each other online (sometimes this takes multiple tries, when technology does not cooperate) and catch each other up on what is happening in our lives. Depending on circumstances, and depending on whether group members are running on time or not, this reconnecting time can last anywhere from 15–40 minutes, and probably takes up on average about 25% of our 2-hour meeting time. Chapter 3 goes into further detail about the significance of this reconnecting time in helping us further develop our relationships with each other. For groups that are just starting out, and whose members may not know each other well, this time to get to know each other may be particularly important.

After we update the group on what is happening in our lives, we each summarize the writing we plan to share during the meeting. This transition into our writing has become fairly fluid, with any group member asking, "So, who has writing to share?" We each give a quick overview, helping us establish how many texts or writing projects will be discussed, and possibly even a sense of priority. In some meetings we all have writing to share, and in other meetings only a few of us have texts. Then someone either volunteers to begin or suggests a particular text to start with, and we discuss our writing for the rest of the 2-hour meeting.

When we share our writing, we follow a fairly regular routine as well, beginning with an author introducing her piece of writing. These introductions vary in time and complexity, largely depending on the author's needs and interests. As the coming chapters demonstrate, sometimes a simple introduction suffices, with the author quickly explaining the genre and focus of the posted text, and other times the author needs to provide a more elaborate context, perhaps explaining the purpose for the writing, any aspects that feel challenging, and what types of feedback would be most useful. Then we read the text silently to ourselves, saying "I'm done" when finished to audibly cue other members.

Early on we did consider other possibilities for sharing our writing. We could have posted writing in advance and read each other's texts before a meeting began, thereby maximizing time for discussion (see Hicks et al., 2013, for a good example of this approach). Because we wanted to ensure that the writing group did not feel like an added burden or obligation, however, we feared that having "homework" before a meeting might cause some of us to worry about having time to read through and adequately "prepare" for meetings. Thus we decided that we wanted our time commitment for the writing group to fit neatly into our 2-hour meetings, wherein we can dedicate time to introduce, read, and discuss each text without any expectation of advance preparation. This decision means that if we have a particularly lengthy text, we typically direct the group's attention to a specific section to focus on for discussion. If we need additional feedback on a longer text, we may provide each other with written feedback outside of meeting time.

After everyone finishes reading a text, we deliberately start talking about what we appreciate about the piece of writing. These positive comments range from overall praise for the content, effect, or genre of the piece, to specific observations about words, phrases, images, or techniques we think are particularly effective or moving. We have found that it is important to begin with praise, so that we practice helping the author notice areas of strength and their effects on readers. Specificity is also important. Articulating *why* these areas are strong helps each of us begin to identify elements of effective writing, as well as techniques we might use in our own writing. Beginning with a discussion of strengths also honors the writer's work thus far on a text, and it requires readers to more carefully attend to what the writer is already doing well.

After our discussion of strengths, we begin to ask questions and discuss our additional experiences as readers. We ask the author to clarify meaning or intention, we inquire about details or significance, and we use these discussions to consider possible ideas for developing and revising the piece. The author is actively involved throughout this conversation, probing responses, asking follow-up questions, clarifying moments in the text, and taking notes to help with revision. We emphasize respect for the author's vision for the text, so that our feedback can support the author's intentions rather than shift a text to fit someone else's interests. Chapter 3 provides a more in-depth view into how these conversations unfold across an actual writing group meeting. Conversations about each text vary in length, but in general last around 20–25 minutes including reading time, depending on how many people bring writing in a given week and how much help an author needs on a piece of writing.

Our meetings end after everyone shares. For the most part, we are able to keep our meetings to 2 hours in length, although there are often occasions where different members arrive late or leave early due to other schedule conflicts (carpool, school responsibilities, childcare, and so on). In this way, we constantly seek to help each other work around the scheduling problems that otherwise might constrain writing or participation.

Sharing Responsibilities and Roles

When we first started meeting, I often played a facilitator role, sending out meeting reminders, inviting individuals to share, and keeping track of time during meetings. But within a few months together, we had a predictable routine and the need for a single facilitator receded, allowing us to share responsibilities more equally among our members. In any given meeting, different members might ask who has writing to share or suggest where to start sharing. We each tend to monitor the time we spend discussing our own texts, sharing responsibility for not allowing any particular member or text to dominate a meeting. We are each genuinely interested in hearing from every member, and our relationships have grown so that we all feel comfortable asking follow-up questions and inviting feedback to our work.

For new groups, and particularly for groups with members who do not know each other well, it may be useful to have more formal roles at first. You might consider designating someone to schedule and send meeting reminders, someone else to keep track of time during meetings, and perhaps even someone to ensure that members make room for each other to comment. These roles can rotate over time, of course, and they can evolve as your group does.

Our writing group has stayed true to our initial commitments to be flexible and responsive to our needs, prioritize talk about writing and opportunities to develop personal relationships, empower each other to choose what to write and how to participate, and enable us to carve out time to write texts that we initiate for ourselves. Our use of Skype and Google Hangout, which allow us to talk in real time about our writing, and a private, password-protected wiki and shared Google Drive space, which allow us to securely share our writing with each other, support us in our online meetings. These technologies also enable the two regular features of our writing group meetings: our reconnecting time, in which we catch up with each other's lives, and our sharing of writing, in which we discuss whatever texts group members choose to post and share in a given meeting.

Suggestions and Guiding Questions for Creating a Writing Group

Articulate and Share Your Goals and Commitments

- Spend some time writing about and discussing everyone's goals. What does each person hope to do as a writer? What does each person hope to get out of the writing group experience?
- Consider whether you are most interested in producing texts or expanding writing practices (or both!). Do you want to focus on composing and polishing written texts, perhaps with an eye to publication? Or are you focusing more on developing writing practices and ways of being writers, so that you want to discuss your experiences while writing as well as any texts that you produce?
- What kinds of writing do you want to share? Do you want to collaboratively study a particular genre? Or would everyone like to feel free to pursue any genre or purpose?
- Be flexible and honest, and keep communicating. Every few months, discuss how things are going. Be willing to adjust expectations for different members' wants and needs, and be willing to allow members to participate in different ways.

Allow Goals and Commitments to Guide Logistical Decisions

- Consider the size of your group. Will each person be able to share writing at each meeting? How will it affect your meetings if someone is absent?
- Consider how often you wish to meet. How much time do you want between meetings? How often do you need to meet in order to maintain momentum on your writing?
- What kind of preparation do you want or have time to do before meetings? Do you want your primary preparation to be focused on your own writing, or do you also want to devote time to prereading each other's texts?
- How will you spend time during meetings? Do you want to devote time in meetings to writing together, perhaps in response to a shared prompt? Do you want to talk about your writing together? Do you want to read each other's writing during meetings, either silently or out loud?

Dedicate Time to Develop Relationships

- Think of your relationships with group members as the foundation for the writing you want to share. If you want to be able to share personal pieces of writing, you will want to consider ways to build relationships with your fellow members.
- Invest time in communicating with each other, even beyond sharing your writing. Provide time in each meeting to catch up with each other, and value this time as part of the meeting (not just as gathering time before the "real" meeting starts).
- If you are a new writing group, consider ways you might begin to form relationships with each other. Perhaps plan some getting-to-know-you questions to discuss during early meetings, or write together in response to shared prompts.

- If you are an online writing group, consider trying to have an in-person meeting periodically, even if it is purely social (like a dinner out to celebrate a great year together).

Plan Your Schedule

- How will you schedule your meetings? Consider planning meetings in advance, so that everyone blocks out the meeting time in their calendars before other commitments arise.
- How will you confirm meetings and communicate between meetings? Will you use online scheduling (e.g., Google Calendar, online polls)? Consider designating a member to send a reminder email or text prior to each meeting.

Establish a Routine for Sharing and Responding to Writing

- Figure out a way to determine who has writing to share at each meeting. This information will help you determine how to divide your meeting time. Do you want to share this information in advance, so you can plan ahead, or are you okay with figuring this out during the meeting itself?
- Share accountability for time. If many members have writing to share, try to monitor the time spent on each appropriately.
- When each person introduces a piece of writing, consider what information will help group members interpret the text and provide the most useful support. As an author, what is your purpose for writing? Is the context or audience significant? What kind of feedback do you want to receive?
- Begin discussions with strengths, and be as specific as possible. What words or phrases or ideas are working or intriguing? How can you help the author notice and name what is going well, so these strategies and practices can be developed in the future?
- When shifting to a discussion about possible revisions and next steps, keep the author's purpose in mind. Where possible, frame feedback as *inquiry*: Instead of telling a writer what to do, ask questions and suggest possibilities that are in line with the author's stated intentions. Encourage the author to lead this discussion, so it is most useful. If you are the author, be sure to take notes to help you in later revisions.

For Online Groups: Determine and Practice Technology Needs

- If you are meeting online, what technology resources are aligned with your goals and commitments as a group?
- How will you share writing? Do you want all writing to be shared in one space, such as a wiki, blog, or a Google Drive or Dropbox folder? Does privacy matter, where only group members may access writing?
- How will you discuss writing? If you want to be able to talk, do you have a preference about audio or video?

- Log onto your online meeting space early (e.g., Google Hangout, Skype) and test your sound and Internet connection before the meeting begins. This will give you time to troubleshoot problems without missing any writing group time.
- Create an online profile, including a picture, on the host site you use (e.g., for Google Hangout or Skype). This will help your fellow group members feel connected to you during meetings if you are not using video conferencing.
- Prepare yourselves for some initial awkwardness. You may have technology issues or inadvertently speak over each other. As much as possible, recognize that these are normal growing pains and will go away as you gain more experience in the online meeting context.
- Experiment in early meetings and talk about what you try. Do not be surprised if it takes a few months before you begin to feel a rhythm and routine set in.

CHAPTER 3

Creating Space

A View Inside a Writing Group Meeting

Sit down right now. Give me this moment. Write whatever's running through you. You might start with "this moment" and end up writing about the gardenia you wore at your wedding seven years ago. That's fine. Don't try to control it. Stay present with whatever comes up, and keep your hand moving.

—Natalie Goldberg
Writing Down the Bones: Freeing the Writer Within (2005)

All of the potential benefits we may experience as teacher-writers hinge on whether we can create space in our busy lives for reflective writing practices. But finding time to write (and time to share that writing) can be really hard. As teachers, our after-hours are full of lesson planning, grading, meetings, family, and other responsibilities. Our professional and personal lives often intertwine, as we experience deeply personal reactions to what happens with our students and classrooms and as our life experiences color our energy and ways of being teachers. This chapter explores ways teacher-writers may create writing opportunities, even amid these time constraints and challenges.

This chapter focuses on how we, as a group of teacher-writers, support each other in *creating space in our lives for writing*. To show the rhythm and progression that a writing group may follow, I use this chapter to invite you inside one particular (but representative) meeting. At the time of this meeting, we had been together for about four months, and over the previous 2 months had begun regularly to share writing with each other. We had moved past the early formative stage as a group, gaining comfort with logistics and technology issues, and we had established a clear routine. As described in Chapter 2, we begin our meeting with "reconnecting time," when we bring each other up to speed on what is happening in our lives, often providing a broader context from which our writing has developed. Then we move into discussing our writing, with each member having an opportunity to share an idea or text at any stage of development. Across the moments of this meeting, group members can be seen using varied techniques to create space for writing projects and practices.

STRATEGIES TO CREATE SPACE FOR WRITING:
LOOKING ACROSS TALK AND TEXTS

This chapter illuminates many of the challenges that teacher-writers face when they pursue writing on their own time. In this one meeting, several members of our writing group mention struggling to make time for what is important to us: Karen is sick, Jillian juggles daycare schedules, and Christina describes a fear of being devoured by the demands of her job. We are busy people. Yet within this single, 2-hour meeting, five texts are shared and numerous conversations about writing, self-image, teaching, relationships, and balance weave together. We discuss challenges and limitations we experience as adults, as teachers, and as writers. And in the midst of all of these constraints, we each find time to share writing with our group.

Our strategies for creating space for writing are varied, and they can be found throughout the meeting. These strategies include deliberately expanding what "counts" as writing, investing in our relationships with each other, attending to our experiences and energy as we write, using inquiry to seek and provide feedback on written texts, and reflecting on connections and themes that emerge across our meeting. While some of these strategies focus on the texts we share, some equally important strategies are developed in talk that occurs during our reconnecting time, before we begin discussing our writing.

Expanding Our Concepts of Writers and Writing

One of the most significant strategies we employ throughout this chapter (and across the book as a whole) is to expand what we consider *writing*. We do not require formal or polished texts at writing group meetings, instead welcoming even raw, unformed starts and ideas. Each member knows that she has designated time, if she wants it, during which to discuss writing ideas, questions, experiences, and challenges. As future chapters will demonstrate, this writing can be personal or professional, private or public, polished or emerging.

In this chapter each group member begins with informal writing, in which we write relatively freely without worrying about detail, form, or arrangement. Karen and Nell write journal entries, I brainstorm using an outline, Jillian begins by writing a timeline, and Christina blogs. This low-stakes writing provides a useful entry point, allowing us to spend just a few minutes but still have something to share during a meeting.

We also expand our ways of participating in writing group meetings. We welcome each other whether we have a piece of writing to share or not. Simply participating in the meeting, through reconnecting with other members and providing feedback on their writing, helps us develop as writers.

As we tell stories during reconnecting time, we often provide context for our writing, even if we do not share it at that meeting. Sometimes the stories we tell lead us to writing in the future. Additionally, as we name strengths and discuss other members' texts, we are actively thinking about writing practices and craft decisions, which supports our own growth as writers. These are writerly practices.

Foregrounding Relationships

Beginning writing group meetings with reconnecting time, instead of diving right into talking about texts, represents another significant strategy. We purposefully begin each meeting with an opportunity for each member to talk about what is happening in her life, personal and professional. This open talk, which can take as much as 25% of a meeting, helps us foreground relationships and build trust, which may enable the sharing of a wider variety of texts. In this meeting all five of us share fairly personal texts with each other, yet there is no indication of discomfort about opening these topics to each other. I attribute this trust level in part to the significant time we spend talking before and beyond our writing during each meeting, as well as the value we place on this talk.

Discussing Strategies and Challenges

We also discuss our experiences *while* writing, both challenges and triumphs. For example, Nell contrasts her experience handwriting and typing, considering the ways her current writing practices both help and hinder her at times. Talking about the act of writing, beyond the context of any particular text, helps her identify challenges and imagine different ways of either putting pen to paper or fingers to the keyboard. Christina shares her own ways of writing when she references her blog, on which she keeps her drafting and revision notes all together. Her blog also helps her access her writing from any computer or device, representing another useful strategy.

Sometimes the writing topic itself can create or limit energy for our writing. By naming and respecting our experiences as writers, we help each other remain focused on our goal to *keep writing*. We might choose to set a text aside, perhaps permanently, if we find that we lack energy for it. Sometimes a challenging life experience can lead us to a writing project, either to explore that experience or escape from it. Other times one writing project leads us directly into another one. Even experimenting with a different genre or starting point can open up possibilities, enabling us to explore a topic from an entirely new angle.

Seeking Feedback Through Inquiry

Across this writing group meeting, we actively solicit feedback from each other, situating our conversations within an inquiry stance as writers and readers. In our discussion of each text, group members celebrate specific writing techniques and use these strengths to consider possibilities for future revisions or even new writing projects. We ask each other to clarify the purpose, audience, and desired effects of our writing. We wonder about possible genre opportunities, and we inquire into the significance of words and phrases. These are all curious, authentic questions, where the person asking truly does not know the answer. The author's responses often dramatically shape the conversations that follow.

This inquiry stance also helps us explore themes that emerge across a meeting. Sometimes these connections emerge immediately as a text is discussed, such as when Karen proclaims, "I'm not alone!" after reading Christina's text in this chapter. In these cases, group members connect their own oral and written stories with someone else's writing, highlighting themes that matter to several group members at once. These connections open opportunities for group members to explore topics from different angles and perspectives.

The rest of this chapter will serve to illustrate these strategies, as I invite you into a writing group meeting in its entirety. Across this meeting, as group members reconnect with each other and discuss texts and writing experiences, we create space for writing, even in the midst of constraints. Taken together, the moments of this writing group meeting support our emerging composing processes and demonstrate the significance we place on each other as whole, complex people who are creating ways of being teacher-writers.

"RECONNECTING" TIME:
CREATING SPACE *BEFORE* TALKING ABOUT TEXTS

It is coming up on 4:30 on a cold February afternoon, and I am tucked away in a basement conference room at the university, alone with my computer. I continue writing, having finally scheduled myself for some "personal writing time," albeit right before our writing group meeting begins. I scan the letter I am drafting, not quite sure what I want to say or how I want to say it. I am glad to be able to share it soon with my writing group, in hopes I will gain some clarity. I know from our emails this week that everyone is planning on attending today's meeting, working around, of course, teaching and child-care and carpool obligations. It is nice to anticipate that between 4:30 and 6:30 on meeting days we will gather online, and that others eagerly await each new arrival.

At 4:30 I log onto Skype and open our group's shared wiki. I wonder if I will eventually post things in advance here, or if the minutes just before writing group will continue to be precious writing time for me. Nell logs on next, her Skype account suddenly showing "online," the familiar green check mark lighting next to her name. Nell is in her home, located near the campus of the private boarding school where she teaches. Christina soon joins us as well, Skyping in from her urban, public school classroom. As we begin to catch up, talk of lives and school and writing merge and overlap, reconnecting us to each other and laying a foundation of talk on which we will soon share our writing.

"It's frustrating that I can't decide on, like, a medium [for writing]," Nell laments, early in our conversation. We have been talking about how we actually write, and Christina has just shared the way she composes as she types, especially now that she is using her blog so extensively as a place to keep and share her writing. Nell usually writes by hand when she composes, but these handwritten texts are harder to share digitally with the group on our wiki.

"Do you edit and revise when you type it in [later]?" Christina asks.

"Yeah, I do change it a little," Nell replies. "When I do a draft [by hand] . . . I can, you know, jot . . . phrasings I want or other words I want to work in. I can put them in in different ways than I can when I'm typing it."

Christina and I continue brainstorming ways that Nell might play around with her mode of writing, so that she can both preserve her handwriting strategies and also share texts with our group. Nell's jottings and later typed revisions are inventive moves she makes as she writes, and even the choice between handwriting and typing shapes her experience while writing.

Nell then changes the subject, saying, "I don't know if I told you last week, but I kind of started dating someone here"—someone, she tells us, who appeared in her poem about dating and loneliness titled "A Comfortable Hell," which she had shared the previous month at a meeting. "So that may be why I'm having trouble tapping into the poem . . . I'm not as lonely anymore." Nell adds, "Except . . . I think like what I'm dealing with is deeper . . . I think I still have to resolve it. But he's the one who poked my ribs with the ice scraper [in the poem]."

"Right . . . I remember that line," Christina says.

Nell tells us she is going with this guy to see a hockey game and do some shopping in a city several hours away, and we joke about the shopping limitations of Nell's small town. We then return to Nell's observation about how her new relationship has shaped what she wants to do with her earlier poem. "It's funny how I think life can . . . kind of call you to write certain things and also block you from writing certain things," I observe.

"Yeah!" Nell agrees. "So now I'm like, shoot! So now I'm not so upset." Nell laughs, and we laugh with her. "But it's still . . . I don't know . . . I think it's still there kind of."

"Yeah, well, like you said, if it's like deeper," Christina empathizes. "I've been thinking about that because the one piece that I started back in the beginning, about my mother, I really haven't approached it. I kind of don't want to, because, you know it means dealing with all of the things associated with it."

"I know," Nell agrees. "Who wants to examine that stuff really?"

Here our talk of writing and personal lives has blended even more completely. Nell introduces her new dating interest by referencing a poem she shared in an earlier meeting, a poem where she described her bedroom as a "strange, comfortable hell" in which she lay awake at 3:27 in the morning, mentally flipping through past relationships. In that poem she congratulates herself "on creating such a great 'space,'/ on finally becoming an adult, /my first real job." And yet, despite these positive thoughts, some nights remained colored by sadness. The man Nell has just started dating shows up at the end of that poem, as someone of interest, and dating him now seems to alleviate the loneliness that drew her to write the poem a month ago. Christina empathizes with this issue, referencing an unfinished piece about her mother. This is an interesting sort of writing challenge, where sometimes the topic of writing cuts uncomfortably close to experiences or emotions we do not want to explore, or where our life experiences alter our energy for a writing project. As we create both new texts and ways of shaping existing ones, we may be limited by the topic itself, or by where the text may need to go next in its development.

Christina then asks if Nell's relationship is "at that kind of point" to do something for the upcoming Valentine's Day, and Nell replies, "I guess, yeah," adding they have reservations for dinner in an area Christina knows well. As Nell contemplates whether her relationship is really that "serious" or not, Christina and I joke that it is okay to just enjoy each other's company without stressing too much over the status.

"Everyone here marries each other," Nell responds in a comic stage whisper, referring to her small town and boarding school community. We all laugh together at her theatrics. "It's a very incestuous place!" she adds, laughing again. "So I'm trying to be really aware of each new stage. Because it could be the last!" Christina and I don't realize it yet, but Nell's joking comments relate directly to the piece of writing she has posted for this meeting, a poem in which she wonders at the dating practices of some of her friends and colleagues.

Shifting the conversation once again, Christina then asks Nell if, as a fellow ESL teacher, she is embroiled with Title III reporting.

"Oh! Didn't you email me about something?" Nell responds.

"I had actually called you. And I got it sorted out. I was—I really just needed to bitch, that's all. I was just like '*Ahhh!!!*'" Christina exclaims in remembered frustration. "I ended up getting hold of another teacher, and she was able to help me out." Christina goes on to explain that Title III covers federal funding for English as a Second Language (ESL) programs. As her district's K–12 coordinator for ESL, Christina had just finished writing a newly required report with her Title III advisor. It is the first year of her school's ESL program, and Christina explains that the report is "not one of those things where they are going to slap you on the wrist if you are missing something. It is just so they can help you kind of develop your program, I guess."

"Yeah. Well . . . the slapping on the wrist sometimes comes in hidden places," Nell observes, acknowledging the significance of Christina's writing task.

Christina's discussion of her Title III report highlights some of the other workplace writing she does. Additionally, just as Nell's comments about dating relate to the poem she will soon share, Christina's work context is also reflected in the writing she will discuss later in the meeting.

Throughout this reconnecting time, while we have not yet begun to talk directly about our written texts, we are still doing important work as writers. We begin with a shared understanding that the first 25–30 minutes of our meeting will be dedicated to catching up with each other. This reconnecting talk is, in itself, an important strategy we all use as we create space in our lives for writing. As teachers, immediately diving into a response or critique of a text may feel in some ways like an extension of our teaching days. By focusing our first talk on our lives, we start by investing in our relationships with each other, on which we will build our later talk of writing.

This reconnecting time also helps maintain an open invitation to participate in the group on days when we have no writing to share, since our first conversations require no preparation for the meeting. Starting with significant time to share our lives *before* we share our writing enacts our commitments that we are flexible, that we can choose how to participate in the group (including whether to discuss our own writing or not), and that just showing up to writing group meetings represents an important way to build writing into our lives. Nevertheless, our talk is still full of references to our writing. We talk about how we write (handwriting, blogging, typing) and how we share our writing. We talk about how our personal lives can invite or block us from engaging with writing projects. And we acknowledge the other writing tasks we do each day. Our reconnecting time also provides a context for the texts that we will share later in the meeting. We each come to the meeting knowing what writing (or ideas for writing) we plan to share, and the stories we tell at the beginning of the meeting often relate to those texts.

DISCUSSING OUR WRITING:
CREATING SPACE *WHILE* TALKING ABOUT TEXTS

At this point we are actually over 30 minutes into our meeting, and already our talk has woven across discussions of writing, personal relationships, and professional obligations. Because of the time, we now decide to turn to our writing, even though Karen and Jillian are still not online. As we discuss our writing, we also draw on additional strategies to create space for writing in our lives. We begin with the text I posted on the wiki just before our meeting.

Seeking Early Feedback and Support:
Christine's Letter to an Estranged Friend

"The piece I have is kind of random," I begin, almost laughing. "Well, not completely random, but a different kind of piece than I have shared." In what feels like a lengthy backstory, I tell about how a friend and I had become estranged, and I describe the central misunderstanding that had gone unaddressed for too long and had only recently been brought to my attention. I tell Nell and Christina that I feel compelled to try writing a letter now in hopes of starting to heal that relationship. "I feel like I *really need* to write this piece," I tell them, "but I don't quite know how to go about doing it." After I set the stage, group members read the text I posted, which is really only a rough plan of how I might write an actual letter to this friend. It begins with a list of questions, as I wonder whether my purpose for writing the letter is to apologize or patch things up or to vent. I then play around with possible language for the letter itself.

The full discussion of my letter features prominently in Chapter 6, but even this glimpse into our conversation reveals strategies that I am using to help myself get started. For example, I do not let genre or content constrain me as I draft, instead allowing myself to jot down any possibilities. I also bring my letter to the group at a relatively unformed stage, rather than waiting for a more polished draft, which I do not feel able to compose yet. I come to the meeting needing a lot of help in figuring out the content and the structure of the letter, and talking through these issues early in my process helps me plan and orally compose future versions. In our meeting I also tell some of the background of my conflict with my friend, and this conversation helps me gain additional clarity on the underlying issues and even my purpose for writing.

Planning Revisions and Clarifying Audience: Jillian's Dancing Vignettes

"Who wants to go next?" I ask when we finish discussing my letter. Jillian had arrived while I was sharing, delayed by a staff meeting but now Skyping from her home. She has to leave early to pick up her children from day-care, so we invite her to share next. Jillian has some questions on a series of vignettes she has been working on for about two months now. At our last meeting Nell and I provided feedback, and Jillian tells us that while she has not made any revisions since then, she wants to clarify some of our suggestions.

Unlike the rest of us, who have moved in and out of several different pieces of writing, Jillian has focused primarily on one core text over the past few months. "The Dancing Game" originated during a timeline writing exercise we tried in one of our first meetings, where each of us chose a topic and then used a timeline to generate events and ideas about that topic (see Chapter 4 for more on this exercise and other ways to generate writing). Jillian had focused her timeline on motherhood, and a game she played with her sons was just one of many moments she included. When we talked through our timelines together, Jillian noted that she found it daunting to write in detail about each moment she had listed. In response, we suggested she dive deeply into only those moments that held particular interest or energy, and Jillian began to craft a series of vignettes that soon focused more on body image and dancing than on her original topic of motherhood.

Because Jillian has not made any revisions, and because we all know her text well, we do not take our usual time to read her writing. We each open Jillian's text from where she had last posted it on the wiki, and Jillian asks several specific questions to guide her next steps. Her text begins with Jillian dancing with her young sons. She describes her small boys "dressed for bed, each of them in their footy pajamas," dancing with "arms pumping, legs moving, and hips shaking" to the music, until she pauses the song and they all collapse on the floor. From that moment of exuberant dancing, Jillian shifts to a second vignette, this time of her 13-year-old self, warming up before a ballet class, her "chubbifying body shoved into a leotard." Jillian shows her discomfort as she compares herself to the (in her eyes) beautiful, graceful other girls in her class, until a moment just before class starts when she stumbles and hears several girls laughing at her. Then Jillian moves to a third vignette when she is 19, this time at a dance club where she shows herself "swaying my hips back and forth in time to the music, hoping the image I create matches the one I have in my head." Once again, she is aware of another dancer, a friend "moving with abandon—her hands rippling in the air, then moving down her body to trace her curves," and Jillian fears "that no one will notice me at all."

Finally, from that club scene Jillian brings us back to the dancing game scene with her sons that began the piece. She now allows her readers to see her more fully:

waving my arms in circles over my head and jumping around in abandon. I catch a reflection in the dark window of a woman in ratty sweats and a green T-shirt that boasts BROCCOLI IS DA BOMB. Her strawberry hair thrown up in a messy ponytail with random pieces escaping the ponytail holder, her face flushed with exertion, her lips pursed in an *I'm awesome and you know it* expression . . . I turn back to my boys, showing them the full glory of my dance moves. Their giggles are music to my ears, and they simultaneously copy my movements, making us three very goofy dancers to see. As I watch their faces, lit up with the joy of moving to the music, I know that this is where I want to be.

Jillian's text celebrates her newer way of seeing herself, no longer consumed with the critical body image she had experienced when dancing as a child or young adult. Her contrast between her insecure, youthful dance experiences and the ease and happiness she now feels as a mom dancing with her children make this a favorite of our group. As we move into discussing Jillian's clarifying questions, I ask Jillian if she has thought about sharing this piece with an audience beyond our group. "I'm thinking about how that [other audience] might even shape the next level of revisions beyond the current one." I tell her I think this piece might make a great magazine article, and I suggest that other group members keep their eyes open for possible venues for Jillian to publish.

"Not sure what you are thinking, Jillian, but I see things like this in *Woman's Day,*" suggests Christina.

Jillian is contemplative when she responds, "Yeah, I guess it's kind of weird thinking of myself as being in that group, because I'm not a woman yet or something." We laugh together at this thought, and I comment that could be a theme for another whole essay. "Yeah!" Jillian responds. "It's a weird thought for me to think about writing for that audience," she says, because it's "just weird to be *part* of that audience."

"Well you could put it in *Cosmo,* if you want," Christina laughs.

"No, not *Cosmo* either!" Jillian replies, easily joining in with Christina's laughter.

Whereas I had initially thought that Jillian would be excited by the prospect of taking her work to a more public audience, she does not latch onto these ideas, in part because the audiences we first suggest do not feel like a good fit to her. Jillian's reaction also highlights the significance of how we see ourselves as writers, perhaps in relation to a specific audience, and how that may support or hinder our writing efforts. It is also clear that Jillian values herself and our group members as a significant audience at this point.

Just as Jillian is about to leave to get her children, Karen arrives at our meeting. Like Jillian, Karen is Skyping in from her home. When I ask who would like to share next, Nell suggests Karen.

Sharing Informal Writing: Karen's Journals About Teaching

As the member of our group who moved farthest from home for her first teaching job, Karen is more geographically disconnected from the rest of us. From a recent phone conversation with her, I know that her principal had nominated her for a districtwide First Year Teacher of the Year award. I invite her to share her "news" with the rest of the group before we read her writing, especially since she missed our reconnecting time. Karen replies, somewhat unexpectedly, "Oh, that I cried in the copy room today?" Laughing at her own misunderstanding, she continues, "Because kids were all fighting and being crazy out in the car rider lot and I didn't know what to do." Karen laughs again, as if to mark the craziness of the experience. "And then they, like, ran away from me," she finishes, a little quieter.

Our voices overlap as we each express dismay about these events. Then Karen does share the news of her award nomination, and she tells us she will have a district interview related to the award the following week. In spite of the significant challenges Karen faces, and in contrast to the way she sometimes jokes about or describes her teaching experiences to us, Karen's principal clearly considers her an excellent teacher. Karen also adds another piece of good news: Her first period class, which has given her so much difficulty behavior-wise this year, has been going well this week. Things seem to be looking up, we comment, in spite of her adventures that afternoon. Once again, prioritizing time to talk about our lives plays a significant role in our meeting, and it turns out Karen's stories set the stage for the writing she has posted.

While Karen regularly participates in meetings, this is only the second time she has chosen to share her own writing, and I am excited to hear what she has brought. "Mine is like mostly just journal entries," she laughs, "and so . . . my biggest goal is to find a genre today." Her voice is hoarse with a cold, which we tease sounds seductive, and she seems tired. "And I think I want to write fiction, because I don't want to write nonfiction anymore. And I do what I feel like!" She laughs again at her own proclamation.

"Are you hoping to find a strand of one of these pieces to fictionalize?" Christina asks.

"Oh, it doesn't matter," Karen responds. "I just posted what I wrote [these] last 2 weeks, because I haven't been really that good at writing. I mean, when I write it's always just, um, lame writing." She laughs quickly, softening her statement.

When we turn to Karen's two journal pieces, we read silently to ourselves. In one piece, titled "Internet, Basketball, and Jolly Ranchers," Karen writes:

> My Internet doesn't work. I wonder why I can't bring it in, and then I remember I haven't left school before six in 2 weeks. I haven't been able to make it to the bank because I leave work after it closes . . . I feel okay, but

I'm starting to get slightly nervous about the bill collectors calling me. I want to say "Hey, I'm trying to get to the bank. Give a woman a break." They don't understand.

Every time I turn on my computer I pray "Please God, let my Internet work. Please. This time. Please." It doesn't, and I really wish I could check my school mail.

This piece goes on to describe Karen's experiences at her school's basketball game that evening. She describes herself talking to "about ten parents," including a mother who reaches out for help with her daughter. "I want to cry," Karen writes, "I honestly love this girl." Karen then describes talking with the student, hoping to help her build on recent successes. Karen ends her piece with thoughts of her next morning at school:

I have to go to bed. Tomorrow Officer Mitchell, the school police officer, is coming to my home base . . . We are struggling as a class. My two home base cheerleaders were kicked out of the game tonight. That should be a good story to complement the officer story tomorrow morning while Tanya explains her birthday situation and I try to teach elements of fiction.

Because Karen has invited us to read both her pieces and discuss them together, we move from this text directly into Karen's second one, titled "An (Outline for an) Essay About Failure."

I really don't do failure. By that, I mean to say, if I'm not going to succeed, I simply don't try. Some may say that that in and of itself is failure. Those people are silly. Example: In elementary school I was a basketball rock star on my island (a.k.a. my neighborhood). I tackled whoever stood in my way. When tackling suddenly became "against the rules" in middle school I never played basketball again. Did I fail? No. Case in point.

That's why I'm thinking about quitting this teaching thing. Because when a kid tells me the funniest thing he's ever seen is a teacher being punched in the face . . . to my face . . . I think, "Damn, I have failed him." I think, "Damnit George. I think you are an alright kid. Why are you a pain?" And then I open another bottle of wine.

And then I think of the people. The two people who have told me that I can't. And I think, you may be on to something.

And then I open an email. An email that says, "Congratulations, Karen. The administrators have met to decide that you are our nominee for First Year Teacher of the Year award."

Karen's writing this week enters our group conversation in a powerful way, especially after her stories about her day. Her voice is strong and honest and raw in these journals. Her trademark wit, such as when she tells us "I do what I want" and when she describes herself as opening "another bottle of wine," seems to help her claim a voice in a situation that has left her at times feeling depressed, exhausted, and isolated. She grapples with moments of significant challenge and also experiences small moments of success as well.

Here, we see Karen creating space for writing just by showing up at our meeting, after such a difficult experience at school, and in the midst of all of the challenges she has faced this year. Karen was late to our meeting because she cannot access personal email or Skype through her school computer, and so she had to drive home to get online. Her head cold, her long hours at school, the after-school fight, and the piles of work that she likely still has waiting for her could each be a perfectly understandable reason to skip our meeting. Not only does she attend, however, but she also brings writing to share, writing that makes a first stab at exploring some of the experiences and challenges she faces. Somehow Karen has found the time to write, and then dedicated the time to share that writing in our meeting. By writing in journal form, Karen chose a genre that is by nature informal and not typically revised, which matches her interests and energies as a writer.

As we begin talking about Karen's writing, we use her texts as entrance points to discuss the experiences that Karen has shared. We do not focus on strategies to further develop these texts, since Karen has stated she does not intend to revise her journals. Instead, we focus on articulating our reactions as readers, pointing out strong phrases and powerful scenes to show the impact Karen's written words have on us. Throughout these discussions, we are deliberately recognizing Karen's journals as worthwhile writing, thereby collaboratively extending space in our meeting to discuss many genres and approaches.

I then ask Karen why she said she wants to write fiction, why she wants to try a new genre. "I feel self-absorbed in my life right now," she replies. "I don't want to write just about this anymore." Karen tells us she wants an escape, she wants to think about other things. She describes these journals as "therapeutic," but she says, "I don't feel like I have a life sometimes," between the constant lesson planning, parent contacts, grading, and long hours at school. "And I'm writing about kids, too." She says she wants to write about something else, so that at least one part of her life feels less focused on school.

Here Karen uses her challenges to generate writing opportunities. At first this strategy involves Karen writing about her struggles, in an effort to articulate what she is feeling and experiencing. Then, feeling a desire for change, Karen suggests her own next step of fiction writing, in hopes of finding an escape or chance to think about other things. In proposing shifting genre away from reflective writing and toward fiction, Karen seeks to create a different writing experience for herself. As we finish discussing Karen's writing, we begin to collaboratively imagine possibilities for her next writing projects. Then we turn to Christina to share her writing.

Blogging and Inquiring: Christina's Solitary Battle in Her New Job

Like Karen, Christina teaches in an urban setting, and she invests similarly long hours in her work. Christina gives relatively little introduction to the piece she has posted, a text she has titled "Identity Crisis." It begins in verse, almost invoking epic poetry, and then shifts genre into a personal narrative/journal. Christina directs us to her blog, where we begin to read:

Identity Crisis

Mouth stretched open, ivory teeth bared,
A dark shadow moves over me,
A known creature hovering,
Salivating at the scent of youth, of passion, of naivety.
The warm, sickeningly sweet breath is at once repulsive and attractive.
Though I know my vulnerability, the danger of being consumed,
My fire extinguished,
I am immovable, determined to be triumphant, victorious, successful.

This is the image I have of my current place of employment. Strange, yes. But all too true. I am in a position where I recognize the overwhelming nature of my job, and the precarious position I am in as a first-year teacher. Statistically, one-third of [new] teachers leave the profession within the first three years, and up to half leave after the first five years. While I know myself well enough to believe that I will not be a part of this statistic, I also am perceptive enough to recognize how this can happen—especially to teachers in an urban setting, where staff and resources are at the bare minimum, requiring teachers to take on the jobs of 1 1/2 people and to make do with 1/2 the resources. It's a near impossible feat.

I am afraid I am being consumed to the point where my former identity is being displaced by a new one. One I'm not quite sure I want to adopt. One that sacrifices relationships held near and dear for far too long for long hours spent on reports and curriculum design, one that replaces personal joys like writing and reading with grading and lessons, one that settles for delivered pizza and Hamburger Helper in place of homecooked, heart-filled cuisine in order to save time for the duties of a job.

Consumed.

For the past five years, I have told myself that I was working for a certificate that said I was a professional. I was willing to endure financial hardships, hours of lost sleep, and a steadfast focus on engaging in the craft of teaching—for the sake of having a career. And now that I'm there, I don't feel like I'm quite there.

Where I am instead is a disorganized, unfocused organization starving for new, young, devoted blood to consume, to fill the long-empty crevices and crags of a misrun bureaucracy. And I'm all too willing to be that sacrifice. But why? Is it for the organization? In hopes of attaining higher test scores, of meeting AYP after being in Phase 2, of avoiding being shut down? Is it for the students? Young adults and children whose needs sometimes seem to surpass the resources of the school? Or is it for myself, for my desire to succeed and my fear of failure? My desire to propel myself into the next stage of my career. Even while my efforts appear to be motivated by the intent to enable my students to succeed, is that desire free of my own selfish gain?

Perhaps I am the creature. Perhaps, I am being swallowed by my career, by my ambition.

There is silence as Nell and Karen and I read this piece, broken only by small comments of appreciation. Tears creep into my eyes as I read, especially when I reach the point where Christina wrote of her fears of being consumed. When we finish reading, our first comments are to praise the strong images Christina has created, both of teaching and of the struggles she is feeling. I share that I teared up, and Karen immediately chimes in "Yes!" Karen tells us she, too, felt emotional as she read, saying she thought to herself, "I'm not alone! I feel alone, but I'm not!"

What is palpable in our discussion and throughout Christina's writing is the sense of precariousness she is feeling, as well as her own determination to prevail. Although Christina's poem depicts her facing a potentially physical threat, from a "creature" with bared teeth that salivates at her youthfulness, her prose allows us to interpret this as a metaphor for the vulnerability she feels as a first-year teacher, especially in an underresourced urban context. The danger she faces, her true fear, is of "being consumed" and having her identity displaced by a new one that she is not sure she likes. It is no surprise that this is the part of the text where Karen and I both experienced an emotional reaction. When we read Christina's piece directly after Karen's journals, common themes emerge and it is clear that both Karen and Christina are "not alone."

Christina's reference to the attrition rate of beginning teachers may provide a partial definition of failure, and possibly one face of the monster Christina and Karen are fighting: the fear that the realities of the job will force people like them to leave teaching altogether. In a different genre, in a different voice, Christina articulates some of the same challenges Karen herself faces. Nell, who has not yet shared her writing this week, comments that Christina's writing also resonates with questions she is asking herself: "What am I doing? What am I hoping to get out of life?"

With so much that matters to Christina at risk of being consumed, and often standing alone (whether to fight the creature or to write a report for Title III funding), it is significant that Christina turns to writing to make sense of her experiences. Her text reveals her creativity, as she translates her feelings and thoughts into poetry and prose. After talking about our reactions to the text, we begin to ask Christina questions, focusing our inquiry on the identity and role of the creature. Christina tells us she is still figuring out what the creature represents, demonstrating her use of writing as a means for inquiry. Rather than restrict herself to only writing about what she knows and fully understands, Christina uses writing to explore her own uncertainty.

Christina also tells us she listens to music as she writes, and she draws on the music for inspiration as well. At the bottom of this text on her blog, Christina has added a note: "As I'm writing this, I am listening to Glen Hansard on imeem [online music program]. And one of the songs I just listened to seems so fitting." She then posts the lyrics to the first stanza of the Glen Hansard and Marketa Irglova song "Drown Out" (2006), which call for listeners to drown out negative voices in their lives. Christina's connection of these lyrics with her own writing, as well as her use of a mixed-genre approach, helps her explore her thinking through different lenses.

Christina clearly uses her blog strategically as a writer, keeping all of her writing together in one place. She takes notes during our meeting right on her blog, which will help her quickly access and use feedback when she revises. In this case, Christina records some of our feedback, including a quote from our discussion about her writing: "Emotional reaction. There was a point where it almost made me want to cry because the writing spoke to me in such a personal way." She also summarizes our discussion about next steps, a reminder to "Free myself to set the issue of genre aside and let it come out the way it comes out." After these notes, Christina writes a possible plan, "Notes from self: Maybe what I can do is continue to go back and forth between the poem, the journal, and even the song. Resolution?" Because it is online, Christina can access her writing and these notes from any device at any time.

Building New Writing from Earlier Texts: Nell's Poem About Relationships

At this point in our meeting it is almost 6:30 and we should be wrapping up. Still relatively new as a group, we spent a lot of time talking at the beginning as we waited for people to arrive, and now we do not have as much time as we would like to spend on Nell's piece, the final text we will discuss. We all agree to stay a bit late to give her some feedback.

The piece Nell has posted actually has a direct link to her previous poem, "A Comfortable Hell," which she referenced during our reconnecting time. Like her earlier poem, this one deals with aspects of discomfort about being alone. Nell tells us that she began by copying a portion of the journaling she wrote for her earlier poem, and she then used that excerpt to inspire this new text, titled "Older Single Women." Before we begin reading, Nell tells us she wants her poetry to be more vivid, and she wants to work with sound and imagery. She asks us to think about these goals as we read. Then we read, for the final time that evening, moving from Nell's journaling directly into the poem it inspired for her.

Older Single Women

But it's SO uncomfortable to be alone. I don't know why. Why is that? The world's full of lonely people. I heard a snippet on CNN this morning about how in times of economic distress, dating and relationship services seem to flourish because people want SOMEONE to snuggle up with when everything else is going to shit. This is a crazy phenomenon. I'm around these older single women who seem NUTS. Crazy. Seriously crazy. They do crazy, irrational things, and I'm afraid it's just because they've been alone for so long that they're really starting to panic. I feel like I look at them and see myself 10 years from now. Every time I see them, I think, "God, I hope I don't make it there." I don't want to be bitter and vindictive and purposely try to trap others just to make myself feel needed. And yet . . . I don't think I'm any better than they are.

It's dark but I
see her eyes take their
jagged journey around
the room. She squints in
the smoke,
stops,
still staring, and nudges me.
"The tall one, at the bar. Green shirt."
I, too, squint above the heads of my friends,
through blue smoke that burns
my eyeliner. I can't
see him. "Yeah!
You should go up there.
Maybe he'll buy you a drink."
She takes a sip and leaves
her IPA at our table.
I shake my head apologetically
at our friends. Guys.
When she and I are
alone, it's martinis.
When we're with the guys,
it's India Pale Ale.
She can hang.

Our feedback time for this poem is too short, and we just have time to tell Nell how much we like it, to name some of our favorite lines, and to encourage her to continue working on it. Christina tells Nell this piece makes her think of jazz, thus speaking to Nell's interest in sound and imagery, and articulating how much she is doing already. We suggest Nell clarify the ending of the poem. We wonder, we tell her, who are these other guys at their table. But mainly, as with Karen and Christina's pieces this week, our feedback is for Nell to keep going, to build on what she is doing. We tell her this is good and deserves to be developed. We decide we will start with her work at our next meeting.

Here at the end of our meeting, after many overlapping conversations and four shared texts, Nell's poem and journal contribute to several developing themes. While Nell's texts are not explicitly about teaching or some of the challenges Karen and Christina mention, her writing still invokes themes of building an identity as an adult and as a professional, being alone, and managing uncertainty about the future.

Nell seems to use her poem to try to make sense of the "crazy, irrational things" she observes her coworkers doing. But what seems to draw Nell into this topic, and what captures our attention as a group, is how Nell fears she may see herself in 10 years. This concern about a possible future is reminiscent of Karen's and Christina's writing. In all cases, a loss of self is at stake. Nell's journaling that precedes her poem ties in with her earlier comment that "everyone here marries each other" and her own questions "What am I doing? What am I hoping to get out of life?"

Like each member of the writing group, Nell faces challenges. Yet, like each member of the group tonight, she has created space for writing amid those constraints. She starts by borrowing journaling she did earlier, copying a portion that had energy for her, and using it to inspire a new poem. Nell also makes connections with other texts, such as her own earlier poem, the CNN snippet, and Christina's writing. Even as Nell is reading or responding to other texts, she is thinking about her own questions, which fuel her writing.

Looking across this meeting, we can see group members employing many strategies for creating space for writing. Perhaps most significant, we each show up and participate in the meeting. We bring different texts at different stages, thereby expanding what we can "count" as writing, and we talk not only about our texts but also about our lives and experiences as writers. We experiment with genre, notice and name things that work, observe themes and connections, ask questions, and practice ways of respecting our energies and interests as writers. In these ways, each of us helps create space for our own and each other's writing practices and writing group participation.

SUGGESTIONS AND GUIDING QUESTIONS FOR CREATING SPACE FOR WRITING

Prioritize and Build Relationships

- In writing group meetings, include time for reconnecting with each other and building relationships. Value this as an important part of the meeting (rather than simply socializing before the "real" meeting begins). What has been going on in each writing group member's life since the last meeting? How is each member finding time to write, in general?
- Try to come to writing group meetings, even if you have no written text to share. Just providing feedback to other teacher-writers is still an important way of developing your writing practices and supporting theirs.

Discuss Writing Experiences, Strategies, and Constraints

- Discuss what you *do* as you write and how these actions relate to your experiences *while* writing. Do you prefer to handwrite or type? How do your ways of writing help you or limit you at different points? What techniques work best for you to get ideas for writing, or to start a piece of writing, or to revise or share writing? Does another writing group member have a strategy worth trying?
- Experiment with different ways of writing. Does it help to write on a blog, even a private one, or a Google document so that you always have access to your writing? Do you prefer having a designated writing notebook you carry with you?
- Consider the role that the topic itself may play in either inviting or blocking your writing. Is it time to put a piece away for a while and write about something else? Is there a topic or experience in your life right now that "calls" you or that you want to wonder about, process, or communicate?
- Discuss what difficulties you face as a writer, with an eye to collaboratively exploring ways to overcome these obstacles. When have you experienced difficulty writing a text or finding time to write? When has writing come more easily? Can you share strategies, even small ones, which seem to help you as a writer?
- Value your experiences while writing and sharing, even if you choose to never seek an outside audience for a given text. Engaging in writing, even if it is primarily for yourself, is a valuable enterprise.

Explore Multiple Ways to Get Started

- Expand what you "count" as writing. Try starting with informal writing, such as a journal or timeline or list, to help you get ideas on paper. Then consider bringing even this early bit of writing to a meeting to help you consider next steps.
- Try sharing writing at early stages, even when a text is only partially formed or conceived. Resist the urge to make excuses for not having more, so you can value what thinking and drafting you do have. How can you use writing group discussions to help you imagine or plan the next stage for a project?
- Allow yourself freedom over genre and content, especially at early stages in a project. Allow yourself to write any possibilities down and save decision making for later revisions.
- Bring questions about an ongoing piece of writing, even if you have not had time to revise it yet. Sometimes just talking about a text can spark enough energy to reenter it again after a writing group meeting.
- Allow yourself to follow the energy of a writing project, perhaps shifting genre or topic as you write. You can always go back later and split a text into two separate ones, or cut out bits that do not connect. At early stages, it may be useful to try thinking in terms of adding material before making choices to delete or limit.
- Read and explore texts that inspire you. Explore connections between different members' texts, or between your own text and music, video, or other external texts. How can identifying common themes or even mentor texts help you gain energy and ideas for a project?

Use Group Discussions to Inspire Next Steps

- Use conversations with writing group members to help clarify your writing purpose and content. What do you think you are trying to accomplish with a given text, and how does this purpose help you think about what content to include? Who is your primary audience, and how does considering your audience help you think about next steps?
- Ask group members for particular types of feedback to help you move on to the next stage in a project. Do you want to focus on clarity or content or sound? Is there a particular effect you are trying to achieve?

CHAPTER 4

"Ideas Percolating in My Head"
Finding and Sustaining Ideas for Writing

> As you develop the habit of looking inside yourself you will find that you become more aware of the world around you. Internal and external awareness interact. . . . The world is full of details that can ignite writing. Look, listen, record, play with them in your mind and on paper.
>
> —Donald M. Murray, *Crafting a Life in Essay, Story, Poem* (1996)

In our early meetings as a writing group, we discussed wanting to enjoy writing again, write for ourselves, and feel like we made progress on writing projects. Most significantly, we hoped that being in a writing group might give us each the extra push we needed to actually *write*. Over the following months, across our first year of shared conversations and texts, we did write, finding ideas and opportunities nestled amid the everyday moments of our regular lives. This chapter highlights some of the strategies we use to create and pursue writing ideas, both in short bursts and over longer periods of time. It also provides a glimpse into the range of texts we compose and how we continue to expand our notions of what "counts" as writing. In doing so, this chapter explores strategies that teacher-writers may use to both *find* and *sustain* ideas for writing.

I begin with strategies that teacher-writers may use to notice ideas for writing projects among everyday experiences. Then I share techniques for sustaining energy in a text across extended periods of time, even when a teacher-writer must set a draft aside to focus on other demands. In exploring these strategies, this chapter considers how teacher-writers may act upon the writing opportunities that surround them. The following examples show teacher-writers who experience natural ebbs and flows in their interest for writing projects. The focus, therefore, is on pursuing sustainable ways of living as writers over time.

STRATEGIES TO FIND IDEAS FOR WRITING

During our first year as a writing group, group members share many texts that we initiate ourselves. These texts, and our experiences composing them, show that we are fulfilling our initial hopes for creating a writing group: to pursue our own writing projects and to help us overcome constraints and actually *write*. Just as important as any text we create are the strategies we are building for our writing, which we share and develop across texts and writing group meetings.

Examples in this chapter show writing group members inventing texts from small moments in our everyday lives, from student notes and text messages, from emails and tweets, and from observations of people we know. We pay attention to triggering ideas or moments, engage in informal quick writing, utilize digital resources that are accessible across contexts (e.g., Twitter, blog), and bring very early texts to group meetings for discussion. Across these examples, creativity is situated within the social context of the writing group, where we help each other reimagine and orally extend ideas and texts.

Capturing Triggering Moments

One significant strategy that we develop is to pay attention to triggering moments and then engage in quick, low-stakes writing to help us grab ideas. For example, when Jillian has a "Wow" reaction as she reads a note from a student, she uses that energy to quickly write a responding text. When Nell is creating a list of text messages that her phone did not transmit, she sees the potential for a poem about failed communication. Similarly, Christina has a thought about communication barriers when talking to a coworker, prompting her to quickly tweet about her observation. In each of these cases, the writer not only experiences a triggering moment, but she also translates that into writing fairly quickly thereafter.

Bringing Early and Unformed Texts

As in the previous chapter, group members share even early texts at writing group meetings. By not limiting ourselves to only discussing polished texts, or even texts that are fully developed, we are able to nurture our emerging ideas through discussion. In conversation with fellow group members, we may consider the strengths of what we have and explore future possibilities for our texts. In doing so, we also share strategies for inventing the text in the first place, which may inspire other members in the future.

Sharing Writing Exercises and Techniques

When we were just getting started writing together, our group wrote in response to some common prompts or writing invitations. These experiences then became additional shared strategies, which we each can utilize and adapt as we continue writing. For example, in this chapter Nell and I both write "found poems," a technique we had tried during one of the literacy teaching methods courses I taught. Found poems involve selecting words and phrases from one or more existing texts (from your own writing or from someone else's text) and arranging them to create a desired effect in a poem (Dunning & Stafford, 1992). Found poems can offer a fun way to rearrange provocative images and phrases in a way that crystallizes or even transforms meaning.

In a way, Jillian draws on another familiar strategy for her writing. When she receives a note from a student, she incorporates this into a sort of dialogue she composes between herself and the young girl. This strategy is similar to writing dialogue in a story, and it is also reminiscent of a dialogue poem (Dunning & Stafford, 1992) or poem for two voices (Fleischman, 2005), which we had also written together in our university methods course. In such poetry, the writer shifts back and forth between two speakers, thereby providing insight into each narrator.

In Chapter 3 I also referenced a timeline exercise that we tried as a group, in which each member selected a provocative topic for writing and then began to create a timeline of events related to that topic. The process of relating events to time periods in our lives, and then considering events that happened adjacent to those time periods, often can spur a writer's memory, calling us to fill in blanks and elaborate on significant moments. Similarly, sketching a scene or a map of a location can help a writer begin to see an image or scene in greater detail, which can also inspire writing.

Informal journaling and freewriting also run throughout the examples in this chapter, and these are powerful writing strategies to help generate ideas. Freewriting involves simply allowing yourself to write for a set period of time about a topic, uninhibited by limitations of genre or structure (Elbow, 1998). Freewriting can easily turn into a more extended or focused text, especially when a writer takes a particular line or idea and deliberately extends it. Donald Murray observes, "Most of my writing begins with a line, a fragment of language—a word, a clause, sometimes a sentence—that contains a tension that will ignite writing" (Murray, 1996, p. 34). Observing and following where that line takes you can be a great way to follow the "heat" or energy hiding there. In this chapter Christina engages in a related process, when she takes a triggering idea from her tweet and then extends it into several narratives.

Exploring Digital Writing Resources

The final strategy that runs throughout many of the following examples involves using digital resources. Christina tweets to quickly capture an idea, Nell looks to her own text messages for inspiration, and I gather language from my aunt's emails to help me celebrate her voice. Each of these forms of digital writing surrounds us in our daily lives. By treating tweets, text messages, emails, and other digital texts as writing, we can explore ways to integrate these texts into our creative writing lives.

TEACHER-WRITERS IN ACTION: FINDING IDEAS FOR WRITING

Across our first few months as a writing group, most of us primarily shared poetry and personal narratives. We are experts, after all, on our own experiences, so generating personal content sometimes comes more easily. As our first year together progressed, group members also began finding inspiration for writing in other places, sometimes amid the smallest moments in everyday life. Many of these later pieces of writing are playful, where a writer had an idea and somehow captured it quickly, in the moment.

Discovering Inspiration in a Found Text: Jillian's Adaptation of a Student Note

At a meeting midway through the school year, Jillian introduces a text that she tells us was inspired by a note one of her students had written to her earlier that week. Jillian attempted to capture the emotional reaction she experienced while reading the note by retyping her student's words and adding her own thoughts in italics, interspersed throughout as a sort of internal response. The resulting text reads almost like a poem for two voices or a dialogue, with the first "voice" being the student's:

Mrs. V,

I didn't know who else to talk to. I found out that Tracy lied to me. She promised me and said her uncle had skateboards and she got one and because she didn't know how to use it she would give it to me. But her uncle never gave her one. And I'm disappointed that she lied to me.

Oh, for the love of Pete. There's always some sort of girl drama that is going on, and everything takes on importance of gigantic proportions, and I don't understand why I'm chosen to sort everything out. I don't have time for this right now.

> And I don't even want to come to school anymore because Michael is always rude to me and he just likes to call people names just to make him feel better. Casey and Erica are rude to me and Tracy. And I feel like skipping school or pretending to be sick because I don't want to be called names anymore.

> *Poor baby girl. I remember what that was like. Feeling like you just don't fit in . . . . Don't let them get to you, girl! You're too smart for that!*

As the letter continues, the student reveals that she and her brother were adopted, and Jillian responds, *"This is news."* Finally, when the student writes that Jillian is the only teacher she will tell this, because Jillian makes her feel good, Jillian writes, *"Wow. How did I do that?"*

When I ask Jillian what gave her the idea for this piece of writing, she describes reading the letter in many different ways: as exhausted, as sympathetic, and even as an English teacher, mentally correcting the grammar. Through her student's written note, Jillian says she gained a more private glimpse of the girl's life and experienced an overall change in the way she looks at her teaching and her students. She says she began to think more about the "hidden lives" of her students, an awareness she had felt was getting "overshadowed" in the rush of grading, lesson planning, and classroom management.

Jillian's *"Wow"* at the end of the piece of writing likely has a lot to do with what drew her to pursue this text. This is a different type of writing for Jillian, who had previously worked almost exclusively on her narrative "The Dancing Game" (discussed in Chapter 3), which wove together specific vignettes from Jillian's own life. In this new piece, Jillian is writing out of a *present* experience, and she can pinpoint a specific moment that inspired her to write. Rather than allowing that energy to pass her by, Jillian essentially reinvents a student's note, interweaving her own writing with her student's words to help capture and make sense of what she felt when she first read that letter. As we discuss possibilities for Jillian's text, we explore options for her to develop it into a short story or a poem.

Crafting a Poem from a List: Nell's Found Poem from Text Messages

At another meeting, Nell also brings a text that is inspired by language found in her everyday life. Nell tells us she had realized that some of the text messages she sent from her phone were not being received, and her wireless carrier had suggested that she keep a log of which texts did not transmit. While compiling her list, Nell says she was struck by how each failed message represented a communication breakdown, and she wondered at the consequences. This idea intrigued Nell, so she began playing with the language she had gathered, drawing on a familiar strategy of rearranging the words to create a found poem. Like Jillian with her student note, here Nell is responding in the moment to an inspiration for writing.

For our writing group meeting, Nell posts a beginning draft of her found poem, which she describes as basically a grouping of several text messages from her list. She tells us, "Mostly I want some direction on how, where I can take this." As we talk about Nell's poem, we brainstorm ways for Nell to clarify that these are "lost" text messages and emphasize the breakdown in communication that captured her attention. Our conversation leads to many possible next steps, including expanding upon the theme or trying other styles of poetry. "Interesting!" Nell proclaims when we finish this conversation. "You guys can take any small idea I have and blow it into something worth trying." I laugh in response and Nell joins in. "Very nice!" she adds, enthusiastically.

We also discuss Nell's writing strategy itself, gathering and organizing these text messages, and what this may suggest about writing opportunities in general. "I love the fact that you're looking at text messages," says Christina. "Like, when you sit back and think about how much you're writing every day, with emails and texts and everything, there's so much material."

"Yeah!" Nell agrees. "It seems like it should be there ripe for the taking."

"Right," Christina laughs, adding, "This would be a fun lesson, too, to have your kids pull out their cell phones and find a text and like, manipulate it."

"It would be kind of fun," Nell agrees.

"It would be," I chime in. "And it would kind of emphasize all the writing that they *do*."

Nell's exclamation that we can take any idea and "blow it into something worth trying" highlights the way that discussing even a relatively unformed draft during a writing group meeting can be worthwhile. In this case, we collectively brainstorm several possibilities for future writing, helping Nell develop this poem and imagine additional related texts she could create. Our discussion also highlights the wide range of writing we each do every day, from text messages to emails, and how much "material" these practices might generate for us as writers. What other items do we compose without even noticing them, which we might later reimagine into a different genre or for a new purpose? Christina's transition from Nell's writing to teaching then shows just how easily some writing strategies can travel from our writing lives to our classrooms.

Writing from a Tweet: Christina's Vignettes About Cultural Barriers

When Christina introduces her text titled "Barriers," she tells us she started thinking about this topic after a conversation with a friend. Following her conversation, Christina tweeted the following: "Thinking about language barriers: Not the kind that prevent people from communicating but other obstacles faced by immigrants because they aren't fluent in the language or culture of power." When she got home later, Christina used this tweet as a starting place, typing it into her blog and then composing a vignette about the conversation that prompted the tweet. She explains that writing about that conversation "started making me think about other scenarios" that related to the same theme, which led her to compose two other vignettes. Each brief vignette focuses on a different relationship Christina had with people who were learning English as adults in the United States. Across the narratives, Christina shows something of the communication barriers she has observed these individuals facing in the United States, as well as the personalities and skills that those barriers sometimes hide.

In this example, Christina uses tweeting as a strategy to capture an idea at the moment she has it, and she later uses that tweet as a seed idea for writing. Christina is using two related strategies here: to jot down an idea that has energy in order to preserve it for later, and then to start a new text with that idea so she can follow the energy of an idea into a new piece of writing. In this case, because Christina used her tweet to capture the central idea that was on her mind, rather than writing a more specific reference to her friend or conversation, she likely helped herself follow that theme into additional narratives.

Each of the above examples, whether writing from a student's letter or a list of text messages or a tweet, represents a teacher-writer noticing an idea for writing and then figuring out a way to take some sort of action, so that the inspiration is not lost. By weaving writing into a found text, rearranging existing language to create new meaning, or quickly jotting (or tweeting) an idea for later, the writer is able to preserve and develop ideas. In each case, the writer takes just a few minutes to write when the energy is fresh, and then brings that writing to the group to develop and discuss. Sharing these drafts not only benefits the writer, but it also allows other group members to develop strategies for finding writing within their own everyday lives.

STRATEGIES TO SUSTAIN IDEAS FOR WRITING

Sometimes ideas for writing are developed more slowly over time, rather than in a quick burst like those described above. The next examples reveal these more drawn-out and complex writing endeavors, where Jillian and I play with ideas in our heads for a while and our writing stretches across several months. In these cases, we continue to draw on many of the above strategies to help us capture ideas, and we also use other techniques to develop our texts over time. These sustaining strategies include attending to the development of our ideas, sharing small pieces of a larger project at a time, relying on writing group members to provide a shared memory of a project, and orally inventing future layers of texts.

Starting Small

In the final two examples in this chapter, Jillian and I both envision fairly involved writing projects. To keep it manageable, and so we have something to share in writing group meetings, we each start with just a beginning writing move. By starting small, we are able to take a first stab at translating our ideas into writing. As the following examples will reveal, these early texts then anchor our discussions of broader ideas. Writers can share notes, rough plans, or partial drafts of texts, and resulting discussions may focus less on revising the texts themselves and more on using these to generate ideas for future writing. In this way, first writing moves can act as springboards from which to launch expanded visions of a more complex writing project.

Exploring Through Talk

Our discussions during group meetings are critical for helping us sustain energy in our writing projects over time. We seek and provide affirmation, and we also discuss our energy (or lack thereof) for a piece of writing. Inquiry plays a central role, as we ask questions to clarify both our draft texts and our broader visions. As authors, we ask about our ideas, writing decisions, and next steps. Other group members then invite authors to clarify purposes and explain how each piece of a text may connect to a larger whole.

Within a writing group, this shared inquiry often leads to storytelling, which may ignite additional creative energy. Asking an author to explain the significance of a relationship, for example, may lead her to tell an illustrative story, thereby helping the writer and other members better understand context and purpose. Storytelling also may serve as oral composing, through which the author actually begins to plan out language and organization to guide future writing. Writers and listeners capture these oral conversations in written notes, so they may later support revisions.

Preserving Ideas in Shared Memory

During writing group meetings, members act both as audience and witnesses when discussing ongoing projects. When a writer shares a text in a group meeting, the other members are able to participate in preserving the memory of that discussion, which can help the author remember and reenter a project, even after time passes. Thus, even though Jillian and I both end up setting our texts aside for a while, we know we can bring a revision at some point in the future and it will be met with excitement and positive energy.

TEACHER-WRITERS IN ACTION: SUSTAINING IDEAS FOR WRITING

Unlike the previous examples, where the writer had an idea and then immediately developed it into a quick draft, this section follows teacher-writers who nurture ideas over much longer periods of time. In the following examples, the writer brings an early piece of writing to the group, and then develops it more fully through conversation and across several meetings. There is often a lapse of time between shared drafts, with the writers drawing on group conversations to help sustain energy for ideas that "percolate" in their heads over time.

Gathering Language and Making a Plan: Christine's Poem for Her Aunt

As I prepare for a writing group meeting in August, my thoughts are with my aunt, a woman I dearly love and admire, who is living across the country. She is battling an incurable cancer, so the long summer days feel like an illusion, and time feels shorter than it should. For the past several months, my aunt had sent regular emails to her friends and family, updating us on how she was feeling, what she was doing, and how her treatment was progressing. Her voice came through as surely in her emails as it did over the phone to me, and I often found bits and pieces of her language floating through my head throughout the day. Perhaps that is what gave me the idea of writing a found poem from her emails, to celebrate her voice and highlight the poetry I felt flowing through her writing.

In preparation for our writing group meeting that August afternoon, I only have the time to go through a few weeks of my aunt's emails, gathering phrases and sentence clusters that stand out to me. This is the same meeting where we discuss Nell's found poem from lost texts (a pure coincidence), so we have already been thinking about found language when we turn to my writing. I ask the other members if "maybe we could just talk about if there's any pieces that really stand out to you, or . . . what kind of form you can see me maybe playing with this?" Then as they read the two-page collection of language bits that I have collected, I begin to reread it myself, highlighting words that particularly jump out at me.

After we read, writing group members observe my aunt's vibrancy, her positive perspective, and the way she seems "really at peace with her life." When I ask what they think about my idea of writing a found poem, they are enthusiastic in their support. Christina points out places in my aunt's language where, "as she's talking about day-to-day things, you really get a feel for what her priorities are, what she values, and why other people value her." Nell agrees, admiring the way my aunt "expresses this . . . almost reverence for everyday things. Like the farmer's market and the sunshine and taking a walk." Nell then suggests that I might begin by trying to find a theme, and she also suggests that I might consider writing several different found poems from the gathered language.

What Christina and Nell provide here, and what I am primarily seeking, is the affirmation that yes, there is a poem, or even poems, hiding in my aunt's words, that my idea is a good one, and that I should pursue it. They also share with me some of what they read and observed in the pieces of language I assembled, which helps me begin to consider how I might go about organizing a poem. Christina then asks me what makes my aunt so significant to me, prompting me to tell stories and describe my aunt further. My responses help me begin to articulate what I might want to show or evoke through my poem. Christina observes, "I think that a lot of the things that you were saying about what you . . . appreciate about her are things that you are really able to convey through her language." I end that conversation in August feeling affirmed that my idea for writing a found poem is promising, and I leave with a clearer sense of how I might focus and organize the poem.

It is another 2 months before I actually write the poem, however. During those months, as I continue sharing emails and phone calls with my aunt and my family, I find it difficult to think about pursuing this poem any further. It makes me sad to work on it, and so I leave it alone for the time being. Then in early October my father calls to tell me my aunt had passed away, and as I pack my bag to fly out for her memorial, I go back to my office for my notes from that August meeting. Waiting out a 3-hour delay at the airport, I begin composing the poem by hand, arranging my aunt's language to find a poem within it. I work for several hours, not sure if I will even share it with anyone else besides my writing group. Yet at that moment, sitting in the airport, I finally feel a sense of urgency to write, to celebrate and remember my aunt as I grieve.

As I write, I think a great deal about my writing group. Even as I struggle to get the poem's language to do what I have in my mind, I know I can bring it to the group later and receive the extra support I need. These thoughts help me worry less about getting it "right" and allow me to dig in and try different things. I finally settle on a completed draft of my poem, excerpted here:

I am OK,
staying open
to the beauty around me.

It is so very nice
to smell spring and
see the flowers.
Sunny weekends
with soft air,

bright sun on the deck.
Time for me to read and write.
Nice chunks of time with my family
good walking, time to talk
sharing stories, memories and feelings.
Unexpected blessings.

I am focused on savoring these days
    strolling Vandusen gardens in Vancouver,
    the Farmers Market in Bellingham.
Delighting in my children and grandchildren
    a hilarious game of Apples to Apples,
    a chance to play in the water at Lake Sammamish.
Remarkable hours of family time.
An incredible circle
Of family, friends, and neighbors.

A week later, I share this experience with my writing group, describing the way our conversations had supported me while I wrote the poem, ultimately enabling me to read it aloud at my aunt's memorial. I also describe what it felt like to still be unsettled in my writing, to have parts of the poem I wanted to revise, but to know that my family appreciated it anyway. It was a new experience for me, to make a piece of writing public and realize that my audience was not listening to form judgments about me as a poet, but rather to hear my aunt's language again and appreciate and celebrate *her* through that poem. So even as I ask for help in revising it, I am aware that my primary purpose for writing has already been achieved.

"I'm going to keep working on it a little bit," I tell them. "But . . . honestly, had I not been working with you guys, you know . . . I never would have put this together."

"Oh, well, I'm glad you did!" Christina responds.

"Yeah! I am too," I agree. "I remember that one day [back in August] and thinking, 'yeah this is something I'd like to do,' and pulling some of the language. And so I already had it partway done, and then I was able to bring it to the airport. And working on it there and knowing I'd be able to come back and talk to you guys . . . you know, it kind of created this space for me to write this."

This poem was probably the most personally significant piece I wrote that year, and working with my writing group played an essential role in my composing processes. Sharing my ideas and seeking feedback helped me build and sustain my energy for this text, even across gaps in time. The writing group meeting in August provided an incentive to get started gathering language before I was ready to really dig into composing. When I then discussed that found language with my writing group, it helped me begin to envision how I might approach writing the poem. This initial energy and writing, in combination with the notes I took during the meeting, helped me hold onto the idea. When I sat down in the airport and drafted the poem 2 months later, I drew on the energy from that first conversation, as well as the knowledge that I could share my draft the following week at our meeting. In this way, I finally wrote my poem and was also able to share it with my family.

Listening to Characters "In My Head": Jillian's Fiction Writing

That same summer, Jillian also describes an idea for writing that she cannot get out of her head. She tells us she met an unusual woman, and she thinks this person would make a great character in a story. "I've been wanting to write from this person's perspective," Jillian says, introducing us to the character sketch she had posted. "I tried to write the way she would talk. . . . It's just like a character rant and I didn't know if it would be the start of something." She also mentions that she has a few other ideas for characters, and she is toying with trying to tie them together into "a few little stories about their perspectives."

The rant/character sketch Jillian shares that day represents her beginning efforts to place her first character, Jo, onto the page. As we read Jillian's draft, she asks us for feedback on how we imagine the character and on whether the writing is interesting and clear to us as readers. Here is an excerpt from Jillian's character sketch, which she calls "Jo's Rant":

> But anyway, I'm sittin' in the front room, eatin' Ensure crap-in-a-can, and lookin' through the winda' to the sidewalk, to see if I can catch a glimpse of my neighbor walkin' his dog in front of my house so he can leave a big pile in my yard—have people these days heard of a little goddamn courtesy?—when I notice this green Honda creepin' up the street in the direction of my house. It stops one house down, real slow and silent, and the two shadows in the front seats lean into each other and stay there for a long time. Huh. Like anyone would want to see them makin' out or whatever else they're doing that a self-respectin' person wouldn't be caught doin' at this hour. The light from the streetlamp is makin' it hard to see through the windshield too good. Oh well. A minute goes by and then the passenger door opens. I lean forward, and squint these tired eyes of mine to see who it is.
>
> Out comes a ratty sneaker, then another one sets on the ground. Above these sneakers are socks much too bright to be flashin' around any time of day, and tucked into those are the tightest pair of jeans I think I've ever seen. What are parents thinking lettin' their kids dress like that? Above the door pops a head with hair dyed the color of my butterscotch pudding, with three inches of dark roots at the top of her head. She looks like a skunk in reverse. It's the neighbor girl, lives with Dog Crap Man over there, and his little shadow of a wife.

I stare at her as she strolls on back to her house like she hasn't a care in the world. That girl is trouble. I can feel it in my old, achy bones. I'd better keep an eye on that one.

After we finish reading, Jillian eagerly asks us about our impressions of the character: "What are you getting from her?" "Can you even get interested in her?" and "Can you like her?" Jillian is most interested initially in whether we think this writing project has potential. Our discussion is lively as Christina, Nell, and I heartily agree that not only do we like the character sketch, but we find this nosy, cranky old woman oddly appealing. Our conversations at this stage focus on Jillian's direct questions ("Did the dialect get irritating?" "Does she say 'damn' too much?"). We compliment Jillian on how she develops Jo through her actions and internal monologue, prompting Jillian to tell us more about the real person on whom Jo is based. This storytelling is fun and amusing, allowing us to consider additional details that may fit into later drafts.

From there we discuss Jillian's vision for how she might continue developing this character, and Jillian begins to share her next steps. "This is like, I don't know, probably thinking a little big," Jillian laughs. "But I have these characters in my head and this is one of them. And another one is like the wife that's like more timid. And when she's by herself and no one's watching her she's kind of quirky and fun. . . . And then there's her daughter, who I think is the . . . girl that's sneaking around . . . and she's all attitude and she's like embarrassed of her mom." Jillian then says she is considering writing stories from each character's perspective, which she can then tie together into a longer text. Christina and I respond enthusiastically. "That's fun," Nell adds. "It sounds like a neat idea if you've got these characters in mind already."

In bringing this first character sketch to a meeting, Jillian is not only getting feedback on a piece of writing, but also orally developing ideas for a broader, more involved writing project. The rant she drafts helps her further develop one character, taking advantage of some of the details that have already been playing through her mind. When she then tells us stories, first about the person on whom she based Jo, and then about her other characters, Jillian is orally composing future versions of her project, which may help her build momentum and energy.

Two weeks later Jillian returns with more ideas for this developing story. Because it is the first week of school, no one has a written text to share that week. But when I ask Jillian if she has ideas she wants to talk about during her time, she replies, "Yeah, ideas percolating in my head!" She then begins to flesh out more of her story. "I had the, you know, character sketch from that old lady, and . . . I want to do another one of the girl that makes a face at her. And I've just been thinking about her." Jillian says ideas had "just popped into my head," which she takes as "a sign that she's an actual good character, 'cause she's kind of leading me."

As we continue talking, we help Jillian draw out and develop her ideas for these characters and how they might interact. "I think you're onto something there," I tell her. "Like . . . when it really sticks with you that feels really significant. Kind of like a story trying to get out, you know?" Jillian agrees, and I continue, "I also think that there may be something significant just about . . . what we're doing right now, just *talking through stories*, because it . . . almost feels a little bit like a way of writing. Because . . . first it's in your head, and then when you put it on paper or when you say it out loud . . . it kind of like airs the character, it brings them to life a little bit."

This conversation highlights the way we are using talk before *and* during writing to help us compose texts. Discussing a story idea, especially when the author takes notes during the discussion, often helps us remember details later, when we have time to write. I tell Jillian about my own experiences, when having talked about ideas for future writing has helped me "return, not just to my notes, but also just to the memory of the conversation" when I later sat down to write. Our oral discussions not only help us in the moments we typically associate with creation of a text, but also as we draw on the memories of our discussion to help sustain ideas over time. Rather than thinking of writing as a linear process from brainstorming to drafting to revising, our writing group discussions support invention of ideas across *recursive writing processes*, helping us reenter a text when we are ready.

In fact it is another 4 months before Jillian shares more writing about these characters or this story idea, when she brings a character sketch of the girl she began orally inventing. It is then another 2 months before Jillian brings another character sketch to the group, this time of the girl's mother. As with my poem for my aunt, there is a significant gap between "drafts" or pieces of writing, yet when Jillian does bring each additional character sketch, group members collaboratively draw upon our shared memories of previous discussions. We mobilize these memories as we orally connect different versions of a text, discussing how the author develops techniques and concepts over time.

There are many reasons why a teacher-writer may need to set aside a piece of writing, sometimes for several weeks or months. Sometimes, as in the case of my aunt's poem, the content itself is the obstacle, and we are not yet ready to write. Other times, busy schedules or other writing projects temporarily displace a text. The examples in this chapter show strategies we have developed for maintaining energy for a piece of writing, even when we cannot continually work on it. We bring early pieces of writing to the group to anchor our discussions of writing ideas, and we discuss ideas for future writing well beyond our draft texts. During meetings we ask each other to elaborate on themes and future plans, and we invite oral storytelling to help authors explore additional angles and possibilities. We take notes as we sketch out plans and orally compose future writing. These practices help us take ideas that may be "percolating" in our heads and bring them to the page. Our group discussions also support reentering our texts later, even after a gap of several months, allowing us to pick up works in progress rather than begin from scratch.

Because of experiences like the ones featured in this chapter, we often speak of having a writing project "in my head" or "on my mind." There are numerous other examples of group members bringing back a piece of writing after a gap in time. For example, Christina set aside her "Identity Crisis" piece for over a year after composing the versions shared in this book. When she did return to it, other group members still had strong memories of her text from our previous discussions, allowing us to eagerly anticipate her newest installation. Similarly, Karen wrote a poem about her relationship with several relatives, with 6 months passing between revisions. I wrote a piece about my halting efforts as a new gardener, and 18 months passed between revisions. In each of these cases, sharing an early version of a piece, even in raw form, enabled us to return later to these drafts and revise. These experiences also helped us develop trust that when we set a piece aside for a time, perhaps because we lacked the energy or time to pursue it, we could still return to it later. These benefits extend beyond merely having an audience and incentive to write, as we had hoped when we first started the writing group. Rather, group members become both collaborators in composing our writing as well as partners in remembering those texts, often helping us reenter a piece of writing when we once again feel ready to pursue it.

SUGGESTIONS AND GUIDING QUESTIONS FOR FINDING AND SUSTAINING IDEAS

Notice and Act Upon Your Energy for Writing

- Pay attention to ideas, experiences, or even physical items that trigger a reaction in you. Try to articulate what draws you in and makes you want to write. Is there a theme you can identify?
- Notice when you get an idea for a piece of writing, and try to carve out a little time for writing as soon as possible. Start with quick, informal writing if time is limited.
- Use digital resources that are easily accessible to help you hold onto writing ideas. Can you use social media (e.g., Twitter, Facebook, blog) or even a smartphone app to help you quickly record ideas and save them for later?
- When you find yourself resisting writing a particular text, talk to your writing group members about what may be blocking your energy. Perhaps setting aside that text for a while, after discussing it with your group members, will allow you to revisit it more effectively in the future.

Play with Language: Imagine Possibilities and Reject Limitations

- Does your idea for writing also suggest a genre? Can you play with shifting genres as you write, so that you can follow your own energy and interest?
- Is there a way to use a found text or found language to inspire you, even just to get started? You can downplay or remove the found language in revision, if you would like.
- Are there ways to start writing a smaller part of a text (e.g., a character sketch, outline, or vignette) to help you get started?
- As much as possible, try to reject limitations on what "counts" as writing or what you might bring to a writing group meeting for feedback. Think broadly and consider even commonplace writing like emails or text messages as fair game, which you can sift through for ideas and found language.

Actively Participate in Writing Group Conversations

- Use writing group conversations to help figure out where you experience "heat" or energy with your writing, explore underlying themes, and articulate your purpose. Take notes or have a fellow group member scribe as you talk.
- Set aside worries about getting a text "right" at first. Instead, have faith that the process of talking through your writing, even when you are most stuck, is a significant act of composing in itself.
- Ask lots of questions when you share your own writing. What do you wonder about a reader's reaction? What kind of feedback will help you move forward?
- Respond genuinely and respectfully to other people's writing. Share specific things that you appreciate, and be curious as you ask questions. Engage the author in conversation about purpose or energy for a topic.
- Use writing group discussions to help you sustain energy for a piece of writing over time. Rely upon your shared memory of conversations, which can support your later work with revision.

Discuss Writing Strategies

- Try to notice and name the strategies you are using as a writer. Collaborate with writing group members to discuss your writing choices and techniques, in addition to the texts you create with them.
- Keep track of the strategies you and other members share during meetings over time. These strategies may suggest useful next steps for future revision.

CHAPTER 5

"I'm a Writer"

Reclaiming Professional and Assigned Writing Tasks

> Your own stories, thoughts, and language are the stuff of writing. . . .One of the first rules of writing is to try to write in your own voice.
>
> —Georgia Heard,
> *Writing Toward Home: Tales and Lessons to Find Your Way* (1995)

Over 15 years ago, I enrolled in a writing workshop for teachers. It was a weekend retreat, and on the first evening eight of us gathered around a long table in a cozy classroom in upstate New York. "Introduce yourself. Tell us a little about who you are and what brought you to this writing retreat," invited our facilitator. A young woman two seats away from me smiled shyly at the group and responded, "I'm Amy, and I'm a writer." I felt struck by her simple introduction. She had taken what often felt like a task and made it sound like art, and she claimed the identity of "writer" for herself. At the time I knew I *wrote*, most often graduate school papers and lesson plans, but I had never dared to describe myself as a *writer*.

My experience in that workshop may speak to many teacher-writers. As educators we write every day. Professionally we write lesson plans, curricular materials, student handouts, emails, feedback to our students, to-do lists, and countless other texts and genres. Writing permeates our personal lives as well, from social media to email and well beyond. Yet too often we do not recognize these endeavors as *writing*. It is easy to create an artificial separation between everyday writing and creative or expressive texts. We also may experience writing differently when someone else initiates or requires the writing task. These divisions can prevent us from recognizing opportunities to build on the rich writing practices we have developed in other contexts.

As a writing group, we share a wide variety of writing. We also talk about the many kinds of writing we do in our lives, including and extending beyond what we bring to meetings. Early on, it wasn't uncommon for a group member to say she did "no writing" when she did not bring a text to share. In those moments, it became important to pause and discuss all the writing each of us had engaged in that week, likely associated with teaching or graduate coursework or everyday life.

Appendix A lists all the texts we shared in our first year as a writing group, demonstrating the wide variety of genres and topics we explored. As this table shows, we initiated the majority of the texts we shared. The table also shows that we did bring assigned writing tasks to the group for feedback on a number of occasions. In Appendix A, texts that are initiated by someone other than the author are italicized to set them apart, and texts that are for academic or professional purposes/audiences are also underlined. The table reveals that even these externally initiated writing tasks vary quite a bit in purpose and audience. Some are directly related to the work the authors do as teachers and graduate students, while other pieces are more personal but still initiated by others.

This chapter encourages teachers to consider professional and academic tasks, as well as other externally initiated texts, to be significant writing endeavors that may be incorporated in writing groups. By bringing these kinds of writing tasks to meetings, teacher-writers may find new ways to reclaim these texts as their own writing, thereby building continuity and cohesion across their writing lives. The examples in this chapter highlight what it may mean to recast professional, academic, and other externally initiated texts as creative opportunities to write in our own voices.

STRATEGIES TO RECLAIM PROFESSIONAL AND ASSIGNED WRITING TASKS

As teacher-writers, we write for our own enjoyment, initiating texts ranging from poetry to narrative to story. We also write in response to assignments, professional obligations, other people's requests, and necessity. Any and all of these texts can benefit from the social, creative processes we use in writing group meetings. It all depends on our needs as a writer, at a given time, with a given text. As we approach even professional and assigned writing tasks, we articulate our writing purposes and what help we need from our writing partners, and we utilize creative writing techniques to play to our strengths.

Mobilizing Familiar Strategies

When we choose to bring professional and assigned texts to writing group meetings, we recognize these varied endeavors as *writing*. Even sharing a small piece of writing can provide a useful springboard for discussion. Often those early bits of writing help us discuss in greater detail our own goals and how they relate to the goals of the person(s) who requested the writing task. Getting started with writing before a meeting, even just a little bit, can enable the author to better explain areas of struggle from inside the writing task.

When we collaboratively discuss our professional and assigned writing alongside our personal texts, we can forge a sense of cohesion in our lives as writers. As in other contexts, we often orally compose language for revision, adapting writing techniques we have used in other contexts. In writing group discussions, we can explore connections across texts and writing situations, drawing on craft decisions that we use in our own personal writing. Interesting leads, dialogue, sensory detail, imagery, and word choice can be just as useful in externally initiated writing tasks as they are in our more personal writing. Similarly, attending to genre conventions and audience, as we must in our professional writing, can help us hone our craft for our personal writing projects.

Making Sense of Tasks and Genres

Writing group discussions help us make sense of the audience, purpose, and context of each text. Spending time discussing workplace texts also helps us break them down into more manageable pieces, enabling us to take control of unfamiliar writing tasks.

As with our other writing, it is critical for authors to articulate what kind of feedback they need as they introduce a text. Does the writer need help making sense of the writing task itself, brainstorming and developing content, or planning organization and ways of approaching the task? Or perhaps an author needs support making sense of the conventions of an unfamiliar genre. We also sometimes bring fairly advanced texts to meetings, seeking help as we polish and clarify our writing before making it public. The author's needs clearly shape feedback in different ways for each of these situations.

TEACHER-WRITERS IN ACTION: RECLAIMING PROFESSIONAL AND ASSIGNED WRITING TASKS

When we started out together, our group focused on sharing our personal writing projects. Then, about four months into our meetings, I decided to introduce a text I wrote in response to an external task. In the months that followed, many other group members also shared texts that they did not initiate. Our reasons for bringing these texts to group meetings varied, ranging from seeking to discuss a challenging writing situation or a new genre to seeking to polish a text before making it more public. Each of these texts, regardless of audience or initiator, played an important role in our writing development and group meetings.

Making Sense of a Challenging Writing Task: Christine's Essay

When I was nominated for a teaching award, I was asked to submit an essay about my teaching practices. The essay would play a key role in the selection process, so it was a significant task to me. At our meeting, I tell Nell and Karen, the two members present, that I needed to "nominate certain practices from my teaching" and explain these to a generalist audience "so they can get inside my practice." The writing task had been consuming a great deal of my time and energy, and I was struggling. Not only was it challenging to figure out which teaching practices to highlight, but I was also unsure of how to present these to a committee that may not have any background in English education teaching practices. Although I posted my entire draft essay, I ask Nell and Karen to read just "the first two or three paragraphs . . . because that's the hardest for me right now."

As we begin to discuss my essay, however, we hardly focus on my draft at first. Rather, we *explore the writing task itself,* which is at the root of my struggle. We discuss the purpose of the essay, as well as how it will figure into the overall application process. I need help figuring out what content I should emphasize in my response, and this requires me to think through what I want to say. It is this focusing work that consumes much of our talk during that meeting, with Nell and Karen sharing recollections of what teaching practices they found significant when they were students in my classes. For example, Karen mentions that "teachers are more likely to incorporate things that they've actually *done* into their own classrooms." Nell agrees, adding, "even as I try to think about what to do in [my] class . . . the things that always pop into my mind first are the things that you had us do." Throughout this conversation, Nell and Karen help me think through ways to focus my content, telling stories to illustrate ways that modeling or demonstration lessons were significant to them as learners. I also am able to ask them their perspectives about other elements of my teaching. As we talk, I take notes, using their feedback to help me think about how to refocus my essay.

Prior to our discussion, I had lacked focus in my draft, which caused me to feel stuck. In bringing this externally initiated text to the group, I was actively seeking support in organizing my thinking, determining my writing purpose, and figuring out how best to tackle the "assignment." Much of the feedback extends beyond my draft text, as we first seek to understand the task and explore possible ways to respond to it. As we ask and answer questions and tell stories related to the essay prompt, I am finally able to clarify what I am trying to say, allowing us to return to my draft and make plans for revision. Thus, unlike in other writing group conversations, in this case we start with an analysis of the task and external purpose for my writing, and then use this refined focus and newly generated material to revise my draft. I leave the meeting feeling much better about my next steps, and much more in control of my writing.

Exploring Unfamiliar Genres:
Nell's Recommendation Letter and Research Proposal

Sometimes, even in familiar contexts, we face unfamiliar genres which create writing difficulties. These tasks are also well-suited for writing group discussions. For example, Nell brought a research proposal and student recommendation letter to our meetings, each of which represented a foreign and less comfortable type of writing for her. In these cases, it was not the content that necessarily caused her to struggle; rather, Nell needed help understanding the conventions of the research proposal and recommendation letter before she could confidently move forward with her writing.

As a graduate student, Nell was assigned to write a research proposal for one of her classes. She posted both her proposal and her professor's assignment, telling us, "I don't really know what he's looking for." In our meeting, she asks if, when we read her draft, we can "get an idea of what I'm going to try to do, like what the actual study will entail." She says she is most concerned about justifying her choices, which seems to be one of the professor's expectations for the assignment.

As Nell continues to talk us through each of the sections of her research proposal, she explains, "I've never really written a proposal. And for me, like the study design and data sources and procedure . . . seem really, like intertwined for me. So I have a hard time separating these . . . things." She adds that she is afraid that she is both repeating some things and not covering others. Once we finish reading, Nell is looking for specific feedback: Do we have a clear idea of what she is planning to do? Did she include the right information in the right places? Is her organization logical? Does she repeat herself?

As with my teaching award essay, Nell is struggling to understand a challenging writing task, and that presents a writing hurdle. But here, Nell's task is further complicated by the unfamiliar genre of the research proposal itself. Nell is unsure of the conventions associated with each of the designated sections of the proposal: What is the purpose of each section, how does each component connect to the others, what decisions does she need to communicate and how? Responding to Nell's writing, therefore, requires our group members to engage in a sort of genre analysis.

Because I have more familiarity with this particular genre, I move the conversation to *genre conventions* and procedural suggestions about designing a research study, using a friend's research design as an example to explain some of the logic behind each element. I draw on our prior conversations about audience and purpose, to help explain the logic and relationship of each part of the proposal. In doing so, I help Nell demystify the genre and recognize the logical connections between parts of her research proposal.

Later, Nell brought a draft of a student recommendation letter she had been asked to write. As with her research proposal, Nell primarily was seeking feedback on *how to understand and compose in a new genre*, one that she considered particularly high stakes for her student. She wondered what type of content to include, how to structure the letter, and what conventions might be expected for language and phrasing (e.g., how to begin and end the letter, how to discuss her knowledge of the student). The draft Nell brought was primarily a collection of notes about the student, as well as some practice sentences to begin her letter.

In this case, we engage Nell in talking about her student, and she articulates some of the reasons that she finds this young woman so impressive. This conversation helps Nell generate content for her letter, before she tackles the issue of genre. We also talk about the context for the letter itself, asking Nell to share what she knows about the audience and purpose (what college? what program?). Then I respond to Nell's genre questions, naming some of the conventions for an academic letter of recommendation. I explain that colleges often ask teachers to assess a student in relation to certain qualities, which may focus the content and organization of the letter. I also share possible phrasing for different sections of the letter and provide several sample letters to help Nell better understand the genre.

Across these examples, while Nell does not initiate either writing situation, she still positions these texts as *her writing* by choosing to bring them to meetings for feedback and discussion. In addition to needing support with unpacking new genres, Nell is using writing to participate in different professional communities. James Gee (1996) describes the way participating in a new discourse community involves adopting an "identity kit" that is "composed of ways of talking, listening (often, too, reading and writing), acting, interacting, believing, valuing, and using tools and objects, in particular settings at specific times, so as to display and recognize a particular social identity" (p. 128). As writers, we are sometimes called to use organizational structures, syntax, content, and language in different ways, depending on the broader discourse community we are engaging. When Nell is writing her first research proposal, she is beginning to enter a community of educational researchers, which has particular ways of writing and talking about elements of research design. Similarly, in writing a student recommendation letter, Nell is participating differently in a broader community of educators, in this case representing her school and her professional self to an external audience. In both examples, Nell is called to use language differently, to emulate different sentence structure and organization strategies, and to craft writing through new genres. Drawing on our writing group for support is a good strategy in these cases.

Mobilizing Creative Writing Techniques:
Jillian's Article and Christina's Introduction

In the examples above, group members brought texts that were still fairly raw and unformed, and they drew on writing group conversations to help them make sense of challenging writing tasks and unfamiliar genres. In each of those examples, the author first spent time articulating the kind of feedback and support needed, leading us to spend a great deal of time focusing on unpacking the task or genre. We used the writers' initial drafts to help explore large revision opportunities for the future, recognizing that the initial draft was only a starting place.

On a number of other occasions, group members brought externally initiated texts that were farther along or nearly finished. In these cases, the author was not looking for help in understanding the writing task or considering significant changes. Rather, the author was seeking more specific revision and editing feedback, as she prepared her text for a public audience. Often going line by line, we focus these conversations much more closely on the drafts themselves.

Across these examples, we also help each other play to our strengths as writers, incorporating familiar writing strategies and craft decisions to compose even assigned tasks in our own voice and style. For example, Jillian shared an article she wrote about her experiences coaching Girl Quest, an after-school running and character education program. Her principal had asked her to write the article for her district newsletter, which would go home to all parents. Jillian felt the pressure to write something that represented her, her school, and her district well.

Before we read the piece, Jillian tells us she is worried about the length of her draft, and she asks "if there are places I can cut back . . . or if there are places I could word things better." Here she is drawing on familiar writing group strategies, asking for specific feedback on flow, pacing, and wording. The draft begins:

> There we were, forming a huddle before the Midtown 5K race on May 21. Coaches were giving their final, and most important, pep talk to a circle of girls with excitement lighting up their eyes and nervous energy causing their feet to hop up and down. One coach prompted, "And remember, the most important thing is that you do—." "—YOUR BEST!" The girls interrupted her with their high-pitched cheers. Despite icy winds and pouring rain that Friday night, spirits were high for these Girl Quest runners. They were ready to race.
>
> For the 3rd successful year, Midtown School District has sponsored Girl Quest, a program that trains our 4th- through 6th-grade girls to run a 5K (3.1 mile) race. Through team-building activities, discussion of important topics, and good old-fashioned running, volunteer coaches work with participants to help them reach their goal. Not only does this program

encourage physical health by promoting exercise and nutrition, it supports the development in girls in [other] areas of their lives: relational, emotional, intellectual, and spiritual.

The text Jillian shares with us is fairly developed, and it shows her ability to consider even a school newsletter article as a creative piece of writing. Jillian deliberately draws on her strengths as a writer, choosing to begin the article at an exciting moment, focus on action, and incorporate sensory detail and dialogue. These are strategies that she has used throughout her personal writing (e.g., "The Dancing Game" from Chapter 3 and "Jo's Rant" from Chapter 4), and she weaves them together with more traditional expository language about the Girl Quest program. In this way Jillian helps interpret an assigned text as a creative writing opportunity through which she can both engage and inform her audience.

As we discuss Jillian's writing, we know she has to submit it soon and therefore is not seeking deep tissue revision. Instead, we talk about length restrictions, point out what we love, and discuss specific lines and word choice. For example, when we realize Jillian is the coach who leads the cheer in the opening section, we suggest she shift that part to first person, to make it more personal. In some places we orally experiment with language, helping Jillian refine and clarify her meaning. The following exchange provides a representative glimpse into our conversations:

> *Christine:* I would actually, in the beginning paragraph, make it a little clearer who you are. How many coaches are there?
> *Jillian:* There are seven.
> *Nell:* Oh, yeah.
> *Christine:* Okay. And how many girls are there?
> *Jillian:* Thirty-three.
> *Christine:* Awesome!
> *Nell:* I think you should mention that.
> *Christine:* Yeah.
> *Nell:* In the first, like even in that first line. I think that would help us. That would be a good . . . reference, too.
> *Jillian:* So what if I said, "There we were, 33 Girl Quest participants and their seven coaches?" Or something?

Across our discussion, we are all attentive to the public nature of this text and the need for it to make sense and be engaging to an audience unfamiliar with Girl Quest. We also want Jillian to shine. As we finish our discussion, Jillian observes that, while she had felt somewhat unsure of her draft, "You've helped me a ton, and I feel a lot better about this!"

On another occasion, Christina shared a different type of "assigned" writing task, this one more personal in nature. Christina explained that her grandmother was in the process of writing a cookbook, and she had asked

Christina to write the introduction. Christina's challenge was to write this in her grandmother's voice, since it would provide a prelude to her grandmother's recipes. As with Jillian's article, Christina's text highlights her writing skills, even as she approaches this unusual task. This is the beginning of what she shares with us:

> Food. It's more than nourishment. It's a source of comfort and warmth. It's a symbol of our homes and families. It's for celebration and recognition. Food is for remembering.
>
> Over the past 80 years, food has been the tie that has connected me with places and people throughout the different chapters of my life. Wanting to remember the faces and meals throughout these years, I was inspired to write this book, in hopes of recording the many recipes from these chapters—rather than letting them fade away. In the same way, this act of remembering also represents my own history.

In this text, Christina draws on her experience writing first person narrative, in an effort to capture her grandmother's voice and intentions. Even though Christina has been asked to write this introduction, she utilizes strategies she has honed in other pieces of writing, such as the narrative portions of "Identity Crisis" (Chapter 3). She uses parallel structure and repetition, and she plays with sentence length, moving from short, simple sentences to more complex syntax. These strategies help Christina achieve the thoughtful and personal tone she sought in capturing her grandmother's voice.

In these two examples, Jillian and Christina approach assigned texts as creative opportunities, empowering them to draw on craft techniques they employ throughout their personal writing. Consequently, their voices as writers come through in significant ways. They also draw upon familiar writing group practices to refine their texts, as they seek input before making their writing public. Through writing group discussions, we attend to word choice, style, length, purpose, and audience, once again deliberately positioning these texts as the author's own writing, regardless of whether it is personal, professional, or otherwise assigned.

While this book deliberately focuses on our first year of our writing group, in the subsequent years we have continued to share a wide variety of texts, many of which we write for purposes and audiences beyond ourselves. We have shared grant applications, emails to colleagues, assignments for our students, syllabi, formal letters, resumes, and essays. As a writing group, we continue to help each other make sense of challenging writing tasks, understand and explore unfamiliar genres, and make use of our own craft knowledge across writing contexts. In doing so, we not only reclaim assigned writing tasks as our own, but we also use these writing experiences to help us hone our techniques and craft. This balance helps us build cohesion across our writing lives.

Suggestions and Guiding Questions for Reclaiming Professional and Assigned Writing Tasks

Welcome All Types of Writing at Meetings

- Make a conscious decision as a writing group to welcome all genres and types of writing at meetings. Challenge yourself to bring any text that you want to discuss, whether it is personal and self-initiated or not.
- When you find yourself struggling with an assigned or workplace text, bring it to a meeting, even if it is in early form. Resist the urge to apologize for not knowing more or not making more progress. See what you can start writing on your own, and then bring it to your colleagues for help.
- Help each other identify writing tasks and opportunities in everyday life. How can these tasks connect to your other writing endeavors? How can the writing group help you engage in writing across contexts?
- Remember to still focus on creating space for your own personal writing projects. As teachers, we are immersed in professional writing tasks, and it can be easy to allow these to crowd out personal writing. Make time to attend to your own interests as a writer, in addition to your writing responsibilities.

Inquire Into New Genres and Conventions

- Collaborate with writing group members to inquire into new genres. How can you gather models of an unfamiliar genre, to help you consider the norms and also the possibilities?
- Explore the logic and purpose behind some genre conventions. Why might a particular audience (or discourse community) expect certain content, organizational features, or syntax in a piece of writing? How can understanding this logic help you demystify an unfamiliar genre?

Mobilize Familiar Writing Strategies

- How can you connect a professional, academic, or other assigned text with other things you have composed? What familiar writing strategies can you adapt or use for these purposes?
- Discuss the purpose, audience, and context of a writing task. How does a writing prompt, assignment, or workplace context shape the expectations for the text?
- Take advantage of your own writing strengths where possible. Think back to texts you have composed and consider what techniques you used most effectively. How can you use these techniques in an externally initiated piece of writing? Is there an opportunity to shift genre, deliberately use organization to focus readers' attention, include an engaging "hook" or opening, or incorporate imagery or dialogue?

Articulate What Feedback You Want/Need

- When you introduce your writing for discussion, explain where you are in your process. Do you need help generating ideas or understanding the task? Do you just need help with revising or polishing?
- Share your understanding of your writing task. How can this help inform the feedback you seek?

CHAPTER 6

"I Just Don't Know
the Right Things to Do"

Composing In-Person Interactions

"I have a meeting with, ah, the superintendent and some principals, to kind of update them on Title III regulations, and also to make some proposals for next year."

—Christina, discussing her meeting with district administration

"I think what I would love is for this to lead to a conversation. Because there is so much time that has gone by. I mean my ideal is that we would both say sorry to each other."

—Christine, discussing her letter to an estranged friend

"My sister's getting married in like 2 weeks. And I'm really nervous about . . . like I just don't know the right things to do."

—Nell, discussing her wedding toast for her sister

A high-stakes meeting with administrators, a misunderstanding between friends, and a wedding. At first glance, these in-person interactions may seem to have little to do with teachers' writing lives, perhaps more appropriate for informal phone conversations than writing group meetings. But each of the comments that open this chapter actually introduces a text, which the author brings to a writing group meeting for feedback. By composing these texts and discussing them in meetings, we find ways to reframe challenging interpersonal interactions as *writing problems*, allowing us to mobilize a range of writing strategies in response.

This chapter invites teacher-writers to consider ways to use writing to deliberately shape face-to-face rhetorical situations. Essentially, a *rhetorical situation* is a set of circumstances in which at least one person perceives a sense of urgency or need, which may be addressed through the use of some form of communication, in order to affect an audience's perspective (Bitzer, 1995). In this chapter Christina, Nell, and I each face situations that make us uncomfortable in some way: a presentation for district administrators, a conversation with an estranged friend, and a wedding toast. We are unsure of the "right" things to do. In response, we design and refine texts to help us navigate these in-person interactions, requiring us to deeply consider our writing purposes and our audiences' interests as we make deliberate choices regarding content, organization, genre, and craft. The examples in this chapter highlight the ways that teacher-writers might draw on their writing strengths, enabling them to compose a written text and shape aspects of an in-person interaction.

STRATEGIES TO COMPOSE IN-PERSON INTERACTIONS

The examples in this chapter span private and public as well as personal and professional contexts. Unlike examples in other chapters, here Christina, Nell, and I are anticipating face-to-face interactions with audiences whose needs and expectations differ in some critical way from our own. Consequently, as we attempt to shape those interactions by composing written texts, we face unusual (and somewhat uncomfortable) writing projects. Yet when Christina, Nell, and I reimagine these situations as writing problems, we are able to draw on a number of strategies to help us compose texts that frame, mediate, and transform our roles in these interactions.

Identifying Useful Written Texts

One of the first moves we make is to identify a text that we can use to help us intervene in or shape a rhetorical situation. The genres of these texts vary, as do the ways we consider using them. As we plan these written texts, we draw on our strengths and knowledge as writers to help us organize or focus elements of the anticipated interactions, and we also use our texts to help us clarify our own roles in the overall situations.

Sharing our preliminary texts (or ideas for them) during writing group meetings positions this work as writing. Writing group conversations then play a critical role in helping the author make sense of a rhetorical situation, explore genres and possibilities for related written texts, experiment with language, talk through questions and challenges, and create a plan for next steps.

Using Informal Writing Strategically

While we use informal writing across the chapters in this book, here we use it strategically to help us make sense of the rhetorical situations we are facing. We use outlining and journaling to help us explore what we want to say and do, as well as how we feel about our anticipated interactions. For example, Christina starts with a focus on content, compiling all the information she wishes to share into one draft. I use a quick brainstorming-type outline to organize my thinking. Nell writes a journal entry and a timeline, and she also uses a familiar mentor text as a model to inspire her first draft. We suspend decisions about genre and form until later, so that we can just focus on content and collaboratively explore the context for our writing.

Playing to Strengths

As in other writing group meetings, in the following examples we begin by praising specific, preliminary writing decisions, enabling the writer to build on what is working. With Christina, we affirm the content she will present, as we help her envision genres that will help her share this material with her administrators. Group members also affirm my decision to write a letter and Nell's to compose a poem, helping each of us move forward with a greater sense of confidence in our genre choices.

Discussing both the text and the rhetorical situation also can help writers rethink a task in order to play to their strengths. Like the examples in Chapter 5, where we were able to use our personal writing craft techniques in professional and assigned texts, here we are able to draw upon writing practices more generally as we consider ways to organize and clarify in-person interactions. Nell is able to reimagine a wedding toast as a poem, which is a more comfortable and familiar genre for her, and Christina is able to draw upon her strengths as a teacher to plan texts that may help her teach an audience of administrators.

Analyzing Context and Audience

Because these writing situations are more public in nature and because they involve in-person interactions that make the author somehow uncomfortable, we need to reach beyond our familiar practices. In each of the following examples, our audience's attitude and purposes, as well as the context of the rhetorical situation itself, shape our choices as writers. Before Nell, Christina, or I can share our preliminary writing, we have to spend a fair amount of time explaining the context for our texts. We talk about our relationships and past histories with our audiences, our feelings about our interactions, and what makes us uncomfortable.

Clarifying the audience is a particularly significant strategy. Both Christina and I have immediately apparent audiences, but Nell's target audience shifts considerably across our discussions. When she is able to focus on a specific audience, she is better able to move forward with her writing. In each of these examples, we anticipate an audience that thinks differently from us, which is another part of our challenge. Group discussions help us consider our audience's values and interests more effectively, which is particularly crucial when anticipating an in-person interaction with that audience. This process also helps the writer explore ways to seek a middle ground, where the writer's and audience's perspectives may overlap.

Considering Purpose and Desired Outcomes

Finally, while we commonly discuss our purposes as authors, here we find it useful to do so in more specific ways, especially in relation to our audience. In a way, we have to balance multiple purposes at once, as we consider both the written text and the in-person interaction that will follow. Because we are writing our texts in order to shape those later interactions, it is useful to think in terms of outcomes. What do we hope our audience will think or do, as a result of reading or hearing this text? We also consider how our text may help position us as participants in those interactions. How might our text enable us to engage our audience differently or play a different role in the overall rhetorical situation?

TEACHER-WRITERS IN ACTION: COMPOSING IN-PERSON INTERACTIONS

As Christina, Nell, and I consider the rhetorical situations in the following examples, we gain momentum by framing these situations as writing problems, which we can then address through familiar writing practices. Our contexts vary quite a bit: Christina's is public and professional, mine is private and personal, and Nell's involves sharing personal content in a public setting. As we compose our texts, we consider in greater complexity the role of audience, purpose, and context, which then inform our choices about content, organization, genre, and craft. We also help each other play to our strengths, as teachers and writers, so that our written texts may help us feel more confident in the related in-person interactions.

Composing Text to Facilitate an Interaction: Christina's Professional Presentation

This first example builds on Chapter 5, demonstrating ways that teacher-writers may find it useful to share even workplace texts at writing group meetings. "It's not the most exciting read," Christina begins, almost apologetically, as she introduces a text at a meeting late in the school year. "I have a meeting with, ah, the superintendent and some principals, to kind of update them on Title III regulations, and also to make some proposals for next year." Christina tells us that as the ESL director for her district, she has to meet with district administrators, and she shares a three-and-a-half page, single-spaced handout she has drafted.

As Christina introduces the text she has posted, she observes, "I really needed . . . to get these thoughts down into some form that makes sense, and I'm probably going to have to change the form. Um, because I don't think they are going to want to read [all of this]." Her draft handout includes, among other things, explanations of legislation and legal precedents, as well as implications and recommendations for her particular school district. In addition to notifying the administration about Title III changes, Christina tells us she has the awkward responsibility of informing them that they may need to pay her out of different funds in their budget.

It is highly unusual for a first-year teacher to be asked to lead a meeting with the superintendent and several building principals. When I comment on the awkwardness of Christina having to conduct this meeting, she responds, "If I was just a teacher in a school district and there was an ESL director other than me, then it would be the coordinator's position. But since I'm the coordinator, that's why it's on my lap." Christina's role at that meeting is therefore complex, as her status as a first-year teacher places her "below" these administrators in terms of experience and decision-making power, yet she still needs to inform them about developments in Title III legislation and make recommendations for the district's ESL program. That complexity alone makes this a highly challenging rhetorical situation, in which Christina will have to carefully navigate interpersonal and professional roles.

Christina quickly steers our conversation back to the writing she has posted, asking how she should revise her text in preparation for this meeting. In doing so, Christina seeks to actively position her text as a tool she can use to help her facilitate this meeting. She tells us she needs feedback to help define her goals, prioritize content, and decide how to actually present the material (e.g., PowerPoint presentation, handout, or other). Then we discuss varied purposes for her text and meeting, what effect she hopes to have on her audience, and how different choices of genre and presentation mode might shape and reflect those purposes and effects.

As Christina clarifies what she wants to accomplish at the meeting, she assesses what the administrators know already (that legislative changes have been made) and what they want to know (what are those changes and what will they mean for the district). She comments, "Part of me would love for them to just read through some of it [her draft handout], because I put in some of the legislation . . . but I don't think that's going to happen. So I was debating doing a PowerPoint and taking the key points and putting it in that way." Here Christina draws on her knowledge as a teacher, considering how the administrators might experience her content as readers and how her choice of content and mode might either facilitate or limit their learning.

Christina also tells us she is trying to use this meeting to achieve a purpose of her own: "to sit down with all the administration and say, 'Look, this is all of the stuff that I've done this year. This is what our program looks like. So these are my recommendations for next year, but I need your back-up here.'" In making this move, Christina expands the purpose of the meeting to include her own agenda, which she differentiates from the goals of her audience, recognizing that she has an opportunity to meet both sets of purposes if she plans her presentation strategically. This is a significant distinction, to identify ways in which the values and interests of a particular audience may diverge from the author's, which will necessarily shape how they interpret the text. She therefore asks us if the recommendations she is making are convincing from the point of view of the administrators.

We then start orally composing language for Christina's text and for the in-person meeting itself, considering ways Christina might integrate her own agenda into her presentation. Christina begins orally rehearsing how she might address the administrators, imagining herself saying, "This is where we're at, these are the changes in the regulations and their implications for us, and these are the proposals for what this will look like or what this could look like." Christina uses this oral "drafting" to help plan a clear organizational structure for the meeting that will facilitate achieving both her audience's and her own goals. By making use of the administrators' interest in the legislation changes, she plans to draw support for her own recommendations from the language of the legislation itself.

At this point we begin to plan and orally compose parts of two texts, a PowerPoint and a handout, which Christina will craft out of the material from the original draft she posted. The PowerPoint will respond most directly to the administrators' interests by updating them on policy changes, identifying challenges those changes represent, and then introducing several responses to those challenges. Then the handout will delineate Christina's recommendations, addressing her own purposes for the meeting and leaving the administrators with a written rationale for each proposal. We hope that this strategy will enable Christina to position herself as a partner to administrators in addressing legislation changes, rather than as someone who comes and poses new problems. As we wrap up our discussion, I observe that as a result of our planned approach, "it feels more like an appropriate conversation for you to be having" with the administrative team.

Across this discussion, we draw heavily on strategies we have used in other writing group meetings, adapting them to this particular situation. We discuss the context of the anticipated administrator meeting, and Christina identifies where she needs feedback on her initial draft. We consider Christina's audience and their interests, her relationship with that audience, her purposes, and the outcomes she seeks from her presentation. Then we orally rehearse possible language for future versions of Christina's texts. While we have used all of these strategies in other writing group meetings, in this conversation we call particular attention to ways that Christina and her audience may have different priorities and understandings, and we explore ways for Christina to strategically connect her audience's interests to her own agenda. Ultimately, we are able to draw on Christina's original draft to collaboratively plan two written texts (the PowerPoint and the handout), which will help Christina facilitate the meeting in a way that allows her to achieve her goals and more confidently participate in this interaction.

Composing Text to Frame an Interaction: Christine's Letter to a Friend

In contrast to the public and professional context of Christina's meeting, this next example is personal and private in nature, involving a letter I was trying to write to a longtime friend (introduced in Chapter 3). Personal letters are often informal, perhaps not the sort of text we usually think of drafting, revising, and discussing at any length. Yet my letter to my friend Angela felt anything but simple to me, because I was hoping to use the letter to begin mending a damaged friendship. As with Christina's presentation materials, I was writing for an external audience who might have a very different way of reading the letter than I intended. This is probably why I was having so much difficulty writing the letter, and I tell the others, "I feel like I *really need* to write this piece, but I don't quite know how to go about doing it."

As I introduce my writing to the group, I begin by explaining some background on my friendship with Angela, details of the situation that led to our misunderstanding, and how our relationship has changed since that time. I tell group members that while I would have preferred an in-person conversation, I now live about 500 miles away from Angela, so I hope that writing a letter might open the door to a later discussion. I want to write something simple to show Angela "that I am aware this misunderstanding happened, but I want us to get beyond it." I add, "I'm kind of looking for feedback on . . . almost the genre of the letter. And whether you guys think a note is the right way to go. That kind of thing." And then they read my initial piece of writing silently to themselves.

What they read is a hybrid of outline and notes, a rough plan of what I am thinking of including in my letter to my friend. My text begins with a list of questions, as I wonder on paper about my purpose for writing in the first place, and then it goes directly on to a beginning draft.

> My purposes:
> To explain? My mindset? My reasons for commenting?
> To apologize? For hurt/embarrassment/disappointment? For ending on
>   this note?
> To patch things up? To create a space to patch things up and recover?
> To be angry? To rise above?
> Dear Angela,

Thinking about you
Since last year?
Since November?
Talked to [a mutual friend] in November
Confirmed my gut feeling—that I had upset you/angered you/embar-
    rassed you
And that explained why you had distanced yourself from me
That was never my intention
I am sorry for any hurt I may have caused you

My text continues as I attempt to elaborate and try a number of different approaches, experimenting with what I might want to communicate.
This represents a very early draft, and it needs substantial work before I can
consider sending it to Angela, particularly if I want it to intervene meaning-
fully in our damaged friendship.

Because my text is so short, it does not take long to read. Christina begins the conversation by observing, "A lot of times when I'm apologizing for
something or I'm upset or hurt about something I end up writing letters. It's
just an easier way for me dealing with those feelings." She then asks, "So I
guess I was wondering if you had any particular inclination as to what you
thought, out of all of those [questions you wrote at the top], what your purpose was, and also where you hope your relationship [might] end up—like
what are you hoping happens at the end of her reading this letter?"

"That's a good question," I reply, "not just my purpose, but what is the
outcome I really want? I think what I would love is for this to lead to a conversation." I continue to think through this possibility, observing that my
ideal would be that we would both apologize to each other: "That I wasn't
more sensitive and didn't think about her feelings in this mix, and that she
didn't let it fester for a year and a half."

"With that being said, if the *purpose* is to convince your *audience* to
have a conversation and/or to apologize," Christina replies, laughing as
she takes on an almost pedagogical tone, "I think that sometimes there
are a lot of things that you can put in writing but they don't always come
out as clear in a situation." She adds, "I guess my opinion is maybe keep
it semi-short where you apologize . . . and really ground it in the fact
that you value the friendship, and you can get at all the reasons in the
conversation." With these comments, Christina helps separate my written
text from the in-person interaction that I hope will follow. In this way,
we consider how the letter may help me deliberately frame a conversation
with Angela, with the combination of the two potentially serving to mend
our friendship.

As we continue discussing my letter, I ask, "How much background,
how much story needs to go into this?" I wonder to what extent I should "rehash" the circumstances of our misunderstanding in the letter, and to what

extent that might happen, if at all, in our later conversation. "Whenever I have something like this," Nell responds, "particularly when it's uncomfortable, or when there is tension . . . but I've also been hurt so I also have a small agenda too . . . I don't want to suck it up." Her words resonate with me, helping me begin to tease out my own conflicted feelings as I write this letter, torn between my desire to apologize and my own sense of injury. Nell's comment also highlights some of the reasons I find this overall rhetorical situation challenging. She continues:

> It takes some time for me to choose my words carefully, which is why, if you have the rehashing in the letter [it] would make sense. Just cause you can choose how you phrase that, and the way you phrase it. When she [Angela] reads it, it will prime her in a certain way . . . like a certain reaction. So when you have your conversation [later], if you are able to have your conversation, then she may be looking at it more like the way you [do]. She may be coming from a place that is more conducive to a conversation. . . . Like you said, you don't want the conversation to be about rehashing it.

Nell helps me in several ways through this feedback: She empathizes with me as the writer of this text, supporting how I am feeling as I write this; she helps me think about what material I should include in the letter, calling attention to the way writing allows me to choose my words carefully; and she suggests ways that the content of my letter might "prime" my audience to understand my perspective and lay the groundwork for a later conversation. When Nell finishes talking, I clarify that she's suggesting I use the letter as a way to frame that future conversation, so Angela will not be anticipating that I will want to rehash past issues in the conversation itself.

Then Jillian interjects, "For me, if I were to get a letter like this, it would be good to know where you are coming from." She then adds, "Also at the same time, if I heard someone else's side of the story, I would want to get the chance to say my side too. So . . . I would think about that. Definitely say your side, because you both had good points about framing the conversation. But also leave it open for her [Angela] to feel like she can do the same. Because if it were me I would want the chance to say something."

With these observations, Jillian complicates Nell's suggestion, as she empathizes not only with me (as Nell did) but also with my friend, exploring what might be going through *her* mind when she reads the letter. Whereas Nell helps me consider my purpose and attitude as an author, Jillian also helps me consider Angela's possible purpose and attitude as a reader. This feedback highlights the way that the content and purpose of my letter may shape the content and direction of the future conversation.

Later, as we close our conversation, Christina interjects "one last thing," laughing, "because of all the CDs [I have] listened to on relationships." Directing our attention to how I should start my letter, Christina suggests "possibly foregrounding the importance of your friendship at the beginning and also closing with that." With this specific feedback, Christina shows me a way to immediately connect with my audience. She also helps refine my purpose, suggesting I use the letter to reaffirm how much I care for Angela. This insight aligns with my interests in setting the stage for a constructive, in-person conversation later. It also helps me refocus on why I want to write the letter in the first place: I really do care about Angela. "Oh, that's a good idea!" I proclaim, "Because it gives me a place to start. Because I was having a hard time with where to start."

In a way, more so than with many texts I had written and shared in other meetings, I have a sense of urgency about this letter, and I need a trusted outside audience to give me feedback. The line of questioning we take, focusing so immediately on my purpose and my relationship with my audience, also represents a departure from how we typically begin our discussions. Usually we start by discussing strengths and sharing our personal reactions to texts. In this conversation, however, group members explicitly call me to explore the ways that my own purposes and interests may differ from my audience's. The discussion helps me do important work, especially as group members push me to strategically choose what to put in my letter, in order to best frame a later conversation.

My decision to bring this letter to the writing group was purposeful, as a writer and as a group member. As a writer, I knew I needed help sorting out what I wanted to write. It was an uncomfortable letter to compose, and I was truly having trouble writing it. What better text to bring to a writing group meeting? As a writing group member, I also wanted our group to be a place where we could think of texts like these as *writing*, through which we could continue expanding our notions of what counts as writing (as discussed in Chapter 3). Thus, while providing the background and context for my letter felt a bit awkward in some ways, especially as I tried to give enough context for my group members to make sense of and help me with my writing, I wanted to make space for a text like this to be shared in our group. I wanted our group to be a place where any member can feel comfortable bringing a text, even if it is a part of a complex relationship or context.

Composing Text to Enable an Interaction: Nell's Wedding Toast

This final example bridges the personal and public, as Nell anticipates having to give the toast at her sister's upcoming wedding. While many people do prepare written toasts, likely even spending time with composition and revision processes, others may stand up and improvise their way through an unrehearsed speech. Regardless, the focus is most commonly on the oral performance, rather than the written text that may or may not accompany it. And that oral presentation can present its own challenges, from public speaking nerves to the difficulty of representing complex relationships to a widely varied audience. Thus Nell's wedding toast is just the sort of text we might want to bring to a writing group meeting to get feedback and support.

"My sister's getting married in like 2 weeks," Nell begins. "And I'm really nervous about . . . like I just don't know the right things to do. And it's my sister, so if anyone's going to do any things it's supposed to be me." Nell pauses briefly, trying to put words to what she is thinking. "But I don't know what to do. So I probably have to do the toast since I'm the maid of honor or whatever."

"Yup," replies Christina with a knowing laugh.

"And so," Nell continues, "I'm kind of nervous about it, because my sister and I have a . . . charged relationship over the years." She adds, "I feel like every wedding I've been to, like, the person's best friend is crying and talking about all their favorite moments with the person. And I'm like, 'well, probably not going to be doing that.' So, I don't know." She trails off a bit, sounding deflated and quieter.

Nell seems to struggle with this task because she does not feel like she can conform to her own expectations of a maid of honor delivering a formal wedding toast. She has shared some journaling with us, in which she provides some background on the tension she sometimes experiences with her sister, ranging from ways they have been compared to each other to ways they each sometimes disagree with each other. The rhetorical situation of the wedding toast seems to highlight the differences between Nell and her sister, Eve, as well as the fact that, at this point in their lives, they do not necessarily share the "best friend" relationship that Nell imagines is the norm.

Nell could have approached this challenging situation as a public speaking or a relationship problem. But instead, as with the other examples in this chapter, she approaches it as a writing problem, empowering her to draw on familiar techniques and written texts to help get started. She starts by journaling and then tells us, "I made a timeline, like I tried to reach for those ideas that we talked about at the beginning of the year. So I made kind of, like a timeline of my relationship with my sister. And some good stuff came out of that." Here Nell describes her use of familiar writing strategies (described in Chapter 4) to help gather ideas for content and focus.

Nell goes on, "So then I thought, well, the only poems I ever write are these 'someone who' poems, which I just think are really—they're kind of fun, because I like to think about the people I like and describe them in a poem. So then I thought well maybe . . . during my toast I could just like, you know, deliver a short poem . . . that I wrote for her." In this comment, Nell references a poem she wrote back when she was a student in my literacy teaching methods course, when I had led the class in a writing exercise designed by Carol Jago (2002). The lesson involved using Sandra Cisneros's

(1987) poem "Abuelito Who" as a model for our own poetry. Christina and I enthusiastically affirm this idea, and Nell continues, "'Cause I wrote a poem like this for my great-aunt when she died. . . . And my dad loved it. My dad and my sister both wanted copies of it, so I thought maybe they'd appreciate it."

Nell has posted a draft poem for our group to read and discuss. She also seems to seek affirmation that reinventing a wedding toast as a fun poem will work and be appropriate for the occasion. Christina and I then read her draft.

> Daron—you've decided to spend the rest of your life with Eve, but I thought it might be helpful for you to get a picture of her early life, from well before she ever heard of [your university] or the fact that one can get a sports scholarship to attend it. To aid you in understanding Eve's past, I've written a poem about some of the highlights I remember.
>
> Eve, who imitated my every motion –
> placed a small hand on her hip and tossed
> her short, dark curls,
> who woke up at 6 am just to eat
> breakfast with our dad,
> their only conversation the crunching
> of the Cocoa Puffs she ate with her
> Minnie Mouse spoon,
> who wore purple corduroy
> pants to school (when she didn't
> accidentally wear her pajamas),
> who started wearing makeup
> and listening to booty music way
> before I did,
> who was fiercely defiant, yet
> utterly fragile,
> who started out adorably round-faced
> and pudgy, like a semi-Asian Betty Boop
> or Shirley Temple, but grew into a tall, beautiful,
> snowboarding/golfing/hiking/weight-lifting/
> sales engineering/Daron-loving extraordinaire.
>
> All the best, blah blah, I love you, blah blah.
> Drink champagne.

As Christina and I start to respond to Nell's poem-toast, we begin by immediately affirming her choice in genre and approach. "You know what?" begins Christina. "I understand that awkwardness. I feel like you've taken a really unique approach to it, and I think it's something that, I don't know, if I were your sister I'd be like 'wow, she really thought about this.' Some of the details you put in here, which I'm guessing kind of came through when you did the timeline . . . it's really touching. I think I'd be touched if I were your sister."

"I think so too," I agree.

"And I think that's who this is for, ultimately," Christina adds.

"Yeah," agrees Nell. "I wanted some things that are kind of . . . like you need something that's kind of like accessible I guess to the other guests . . . It's mostly for her, but I don't want everybody to be bored out of their mind."

In this exchange, Christina places herself in the role of Nell's sister, imagining how she might respond if someone wrote such a poem for her. Christina's comments help Nell start to clarify her audience, focusing her attention on the bride. Then as we read through the poem again, Nell asks us to help further clarify her audience and their expectations for a toast: "Is it interesting enough like for people who don't know her as well? And . . . do you think the length would be appropriate?" These questions reveal Nell's awareness of her varied audience, which includes both her sister and the rest of the wedding guests.

While Nell initially addressed this toast to the groom, perhaps as a way of justifying her approach and allowing her to keep the poem in the third person ("Eve, who"—to follow Cisneros' model), at no point in our discussions do we reference Daron as the primary audience. As we continue discussing Nell's poem, we also talk more about other expectations of a wedding toast and the *conventions of the rhetorical situation* (the wedding). We observe that wedding toasts are commonly funny and nice, intended to make the person being toasted feel good at his/her wedding. This conversation seems to address Nell's concerns about whether her toast is appropriate. By discussing the purpose of the toast, we are able to consider ways that Nell's purpose (as writer) and her sister's purpose (as audience) can be aligned.

Christina and I also comment on some of the specific details Nell has in her draft. We observe how personal the beginning of the poem is, packed with images and memories and observations. We notice that from there it jumps to the present, and we suggest that Nell could develop the middle section a bit more. This missing "middle part" likely aligns with the part of Nell and Eve's relationship that has become more challenging, but we note that the emphasis on the early days can allow Nell to get by with adding only a few more details, just to connect childhood to the present time period. This will enable Nell to highlight tender memories and avoid those themes that might be less comfortable.

Across our conversations, Nell continues to consider this pending in-person interaction, when she must publicly toast her sister, as an opportunity to draw on her composing strategies. In doing so, she is able to transform the toast from a challenging genre (personal speech) into a genre that she finds fun and accessible (poem). Nell has shared several poems this year in our writing group, so she is drawing deliberately on her writing strengths. Christina and I affirm Nell's choice of genre and help clarify her audience and purpose. This process allows us to assess if the toast is effective (Is it funny? Is it nice?).

It is not until the following month that we are able to hear how the toast went. At that time, Nell brings her toast to our meeting so we can read what she shared at the wedding. She tells us that she may still polish it a bit, so she can print it out and give it to her sister as a gift. Reading Nell's "final" version of her toast provides a view into the revisions she made before orally delivering it at her sister's wedding:

My little sister, Eve,
who is the child in our family with
the Caucasian eyes and nose,
who used to imitate my every motion—
who would place a small
hand on her hip and toss
her short, dark curls,
who, as a child, woke up at 6 am just to have
a silent breakfast with our dad,
their only conversation the crunching
of Cocoa Puffs as she ate with her
Minnie Mouse spoon, who wore
purple corduroy pants
to school when she didn't accidentally wear
her pajamas.

My little sister, Eve,
who pulled me aside before her 3rd-grade Spring Concert
to ask for advice on how to clap "the cool way,"
who would play games with me
when we should have been in bed,
who, when our mom checked on us,
could fake a deep sleep well enough
to win an Academy Award,
who, when she was scared
that the tiny frogs under her bed were trying
to bite her toes, used to ask
me to crawl into bed with her,
who loved Koosh Balls and Gak,
Ducktales and *Anne of Green Gables*,
who started wearing makeup and listening
to Will Smith and Lauren Hill

way before I did,
who, when I would go to her for help
with my hair before a date or dance,
would roll her eyes, hold up a lock of my hair,
and sigh, "That's because you need to
use product, Nell,"
who released her teenaged anger by
slamming
her bedroom door so often that
our parents removed her door completely,
whom I still call when I need serious advice.

My little sister, Eve,
who started out adorably
round-faced and pudgy,
like a semi-Asian
Shirley Temple,
but has grown into a tall,
beautiful, organized,
snowboarding/weightlifting/
volleyball-spiking/golfing/hiking/
sales-engineering/Daron-loving
extraordinaire.

Nell clearly made use of writing group feedback in revising her toast. In this enacted version, Nell has changed from the third person "Eve, who" to the first person "My little sister, Eve," and she has dropped the introduction addressing it to Daron. In this way, Nell has targeted her sister as her primary audience, focusing the poem on their shared relationship. This final version is personal and funny, and it provides tender images of the sisters at different points in their childhood and young adult lives. There are moments when Nell does compare her sister and herself, showing how different they are (her sister wearing makeup and "product" in her hair, for example), but even these comparisons fit the expectations of friendly humor, designed to make her sister and others laugh comfortably. When Nell ends the poem, she ends it with a toast-worthy list of her sister's strengths and accomplishments, and she references her sister's love for her new husband.

In many ways this text helps Nell not only deliver a toast, but also *be* the maid of honor in ways that feel comfortable to her. Even though she may not feel like she and her sister always share a conventional relationship, Nell has written a poem-toast that defines their relationship in ways that are tender and humorous, enabling her to be the toast-giving maid of honor in her sister's wedding.

Taken together, the three examples in this chapter provide a different way of thinking about potentials for teachers' writing. The texts are highly contextualized and less likely, therefore, to become models in classroom writing lessons, since they are so specific to particular writing contexts. And yet the experiences we have while crafting these texts, especially as we grapple with audience and purpose, and as we consider the ways our writing can frame future interactions, can inform our future writing practices and pedagogies.

Teachers are often encouraged to write to participate in discussions in the field, toward having a voice in shaping conversations about education (Check, 2002; McEntee, 1998; Whitney et al., 2012; Whitney et al., 2014). The examples in this chapter provide useful models for how to think about the relationship between a written text and an in-person interaction, highlighting ways that teacher-writers may deliberately compose texts in order to facilitate or frame particular interactions, or enable themselves to take certain roles. As the teacher-writers in this chapter collaborate to analyze and then respond to complex rhetorical situations, they compose written texts and shape aspects of the corresponding in-person interactions. By intentionally *recasting challenging in-person interactions as writing problems*, teacher-writers may find it easier to use familiar, inventive writing strategies and play to their strengths.

When we purposefully compose a text that will mediate an in-person rhetorical situation, we also invent ways of being in those situations. For example, as we orally invent Christina's PowerPoint and handout, and as she considers what content to include and how to connect her goals with her administrators', she can be seen inventing a way of being a leader and an ESL coordinator, even as a first-year teacher. As I consider how to frame my letter and what content to include, I am composing a way of being a friend, even in the midst of a long-distance misunderstanding. And as we discuss Nell's wedding toast, and as she considers how to craft her poem, she can be seen figuring out a way to be a sister and a maid of honor. This theme is explored in more detail in Chapter 7.

SUGGESTIONS AND GUIDING QUESTIONS FOR
COMPOSING IN-PERSON INTERACTIONS

Identify and Analyze Your Audience, Purpose, and Attitude

- Who are the various members of the audience for the in-person interaction? If the audience is varied, how do these audiences relate to each other, and how might you determine your focal audience?
- Discuss your attitude toward your audience. Are there feelings you bring into this interaction, which may constrain your writing? If this is the case, is there a way you can shift your focus to more neutral ground?
- What goals or interests might your audience have, relative to you or to the content you will present? Are there significant ways that your audience's interests or goals may differ from your own? Is there a way you can connect your audience's goals with your own?
- What is your primary purpose for this interaction? How can a written text help you meet some aspects of this purpose?

Identify and Plan a Relevant Text

- Is there a written text that you can share with your audience, which will help you meet some of your goals (or lay the groundwork) for the in-person interaction?
- What roles might your text play in the situation? Is there a way to communicate with your audience through writing, to take some of the pressure off an in-person interaction?
- Try out informal or simple ways to begin writing your text. Journal about your topic or your audience, or try making a list of what you want to cover.
- Think broadly about genre and form. Is there a particular genre that may feel most comfortable to you or to your audience? Would two different genres be needed to help meet two different goals or purposes?
- Think about content and organization as they relate to your audience. Is there particular content that your audience will expect to read or hear? How can you strategically organize your content so that your audience will be most receptive to it and so that it aligns with your overall purpose?

Discuss Your Early Writing and Context

- When you share with your writing group, begin by providing background context for the rhetorical situation and the text you are sharing. What information does your writing group need to know about the in-person interaction associated with this text? What aspects of that in-person interaction are most challenging for you?
- Share what kind of help you are seeking from your writing group. What aspects of your written text do you need to target in your discussion?

- Use your discussion to help you articulate your audience, purpose, and context. Writing group members can ask clarifying questions to help you with this process.
- Ask writing group members for feedback about what is working in your first draft. What is their reaction to the content, genre, or approach you are trying?
- Orally experiment with new language and approaches. It may be useful to have someone jot notes as you and group members talk, to capture the language that is orally invented.

Play to Your Strengths

- Ask your group members to help you think of ways to play to your strengths as a writer and a teacher, perhaps helping you deliberately think of your text as a particular type of writing or teaching task.
- Think about what genres or writing strategies feel comfortable to you. Is there a way to incorporate or adapt these into your text?

CHAPTER 7

"I Look at Them and See Myself"

Composing Identities and Ways of Being

> We are a species that needs and wants to understand who we are. Sheep lice do not seem to share this longing, which is one reason why they write so very little.
>
> —Anne Lamott,
> *Bird by Bird: Some Instructions on Writing and Life* (1995)

One of the benefits of writing together is the shared memory a writing group can establish, so that we eagerly await new developments in each other's writing each time we meet. It can be a bit like looking forward to the next episode of a favorite television comedy or drama. What themes or new ideas will emerge?

This chapter follows three of the texts initially discussed in Chapter 3 into our next writing group meeting, 2 weeks later: Nell's poem "Older Single Women," Karen's journaling about teaching, and Christina's epic poem/personal narrative "Identity Crisis." As these next layers of writing unfold, it may be tempting to focus only on how those texts themselves develop, as each teacher-writer adds to her story and refines her craft. While this chapter provides a view into the ongoing invention (and reinvention) of these texts, it also explores what is potentially an even more intriguing question: *What do our textual compositions enable us to create about ourselves as individuals?* Or, to put it another way, *How might we compose identities and ways of being through our writing?*

The examples in this chapter are designed to help teacher-writers notice what they compose as writers, including and extending beyond the texts they create. As Nell, Christina, and Karen craft texts, they compose, among other things, identities as writers, individuals, partners, parents, teachers, and writing group members. They also compose ways of persevering, remembering, and making decisions.

As noted in Chapter 1, Bob Yagelski (2009, 2011, 2012) points to the significance of the experiences writers have *as they write*, highlighting the transformative potential of the act of writing itself. Sometimes it is not the text that is created, or the lesson plan it enables, that really matters most to the teacher-writer. Sometimes the experiences we have throughout the composition process, including both the private moments of writing and the more social interactions of discussing texts and ideas, are the more significant creative acts.

HOW WE COMPOSE IDENTITIES AND WAYS OF BEING

The examples in this chapter follow Nell, Karen, and Christina as they compose personally significant texts through writing and collaborative talk. In some cases they write themselves as characters in their texts, using genre and voice to strategically portray themselves in certain ways. They weave talk and writing together, exploring experiences and relationships and then portraying these in deliberate ways in their texts. Their writing processes and experiences enable them to compose not only meaningful texts, but also identities and ways of being in the world.

Including the Self as a Character

Each of the examples in this chapter involves the author telling some sort of story, either in the writing itself or in discussion during a meeting. While storytelling has been featured across other chapters in this book, this chapter goes a step further to consider ways writers may actively position themselves as characters in their stories. By describing the self in certain ways, perhaps in action or in relation to other characters or challenges, the author uses writing to compose aspects of identity. In Christina's writing, for example, she depicts herself as a hero and warrior, even as she acknowledges her vulnerability and the obstacles that loom in front of her.

Similarly, oral storytelling figures prominently in this chapter. Nell and Karen entertain us with performative, humorous accounts of experiences related to their writing, and they have us laughing as they relay events involving colleagues and students. The way Nell and Karen tell these stories also involves them shaping their own identities, relative to the other characters and events they describe. Karen positions herself as a survivor, one of the teachers who is making it and can therefore almost laugh at the challenges she has faced. Nell describes a few colleagues' "crazy" behavior, inviting good-natured laughing at various antics while also contrasting her own rational and detached role in the stories. Telling stories, orally and in writing, enables these teacher-writers to highlight the humor and discomfort they face. The way they show themselves in these moments, through descriptive statements and characterization, also represents a means of composing an identity or way of being in those narratives.

Using Genre Strategically

Each of the texts in this chapter could easily be imagined as a simple journal entry or written reflection. Yet each of the writers plays with a different genre in order to explore their topic from a less conventional angle. As Nell and Christina turn to poetry and Karen writes mock emails, they play with figurative language, imagery, and tone. They use genre to experiment with showing the conflicts they experience rather than attempting to directly explain these, thereby following the old writing maxim: "Don't tell, but show" (e.g., see Goldberg, 2005, p. 75). It is through these different genre choices that they are able to write themselves into their texts, either as explicit characters (Christina's solitary hero) or observers (Nell's rational, detached role).

Genre also links to these authors' use of writing as a form of inquiry. Christina explicitly notes that she is using writing to work through questions, to help her decide on a course of action. Again, rather than approaching this decision-making solely through journaling or reflective writing, Christina moves between a poem and narrative, allowing herself to give her complex tangle of emotions a form as a looming creature. Nell, too, shifts from a quick journal entry into her poem, in an effort to show herself in relation to her colleagues and inquire into her worries that she may one day mirror their behaviors.

Using Talk to Inform Writing and Inquiry

As in other chapters, we also talk about our purposes and our experiences while writing. In the following examples, our conversations often extend well beyond the texts. Sometimes group members orally describe their own roles or actions, thereby identifying or positioning themselves in specific ways. Other times group members talk through their purposes for writing, which helps them articulate additional significant inventive work they are doing.

As we discuss our writing, we offer different kinds of support to each other as writers and as people, depending on what a given text and conversation seem to need. We ask questions, we relate ideas to our own experiences, we laugh at funny stories, and we tell each other to "write that down!" when we hear something that seems like it belongs in the text. Writing group conversations help writers follow their energy, elaborate stories, ponder possibilities, and recognize progress. Each of these moves helps the writer shape her text and also supports the writer in exploring the significance of that text, perhaps in relation to her understanding of self or her ways of being in the world.

Expanding Notions of Teacher-Writers

The examples in this chapter also expand traditional notions of teacher-writers. As introduced in Chapter 1, teachers' writing endeavors are often seen primarily as a means for developing their teaching practices, with an emphasis on teachers creating texts and practices that are in service to their students and their own professional lives. It is no wonder that writing, when positioned primarily in this way, sometimes can feel like one more expectation placed on teachers, a well-intentioned "log" that might extinguish rather than fuel their fires. Yet the teacher-writers featured in this chapter are not merely writing to be better teachers, but to explore relationships and make sense of experiences that matter to them. The texts they create have personal significance, and their experiences while writing are equally meaningful. Nell, Karen, and Christina are exploring who they are, how they relate to others, what they value, and what they hope for the future. They engage in the sort of potentially transformative experiences *while writing* and talking about writing that Bob Yagelski describes—and I argue that these other outcomes, and the strategies that enable them, are often even more important than their texts.

TEACHER-WRITERS IN ACTION: COMPOSING IDENTITIES AND WAYS OF BEING

In Chapter 3 we encountered Nell's early draft of her poem "Older Single Women," Christina's first draft of "Identity Crisis," and Karen's journal entries about her teaching experiences. Now, we follow each of these authors into the next meeting, 2 weeks later, when she shares a next layer of her text or idea. Nell brings a revised poem, and Christina shares a next installment of her text. Karen combines her interest in shifting genre and her passion about teaching to begin a longer, multigenre text.

Across the following examples, this chapter seeks to help teacher-writers consider the significance of our experiences *while* writing and discussing writing, regardless of what we decide to do with a given text. As Nell, Karen, and Christina revisit and expand their earlier drafts, they recast experiences and ideas using different genres to make new sense of personal experiences. In doing so, they can be seen composing not only texts, but identities and ways of being in the world.

Contrasting Self with Others: Nell's "Older Single Women"

When Nell shared her first draft of her poem "Older Single Women" (Chapter 3), she was attempting to make sense of some of the dating behavior she observed among her friends and colleagues. Nell's new home is several hours from where she grew up, near the campus of her boarding school job. She can walk to her classroom but must drive to get off campus and into town. Many of her friends are her colleagues, and, not surprisingly, many dating relationships develop among faculty.

Nell begins by reintroducing her poem to us, providing a quick summary of how she has revised it since our previous meeting. "I made a couple of changes based on what you guys were saying," she explains. She clarified the identities of the other people in the poem and tried to provide "a little bit of background information" to make the context more clear. She notes that she is "having trouble jumping between the two different scenes" of the bar and school, and her comments help us consider what kind of feedback she may find most useful.

Nell also shares a bit of her writing process with us, explaining that as she worked on the poem she was thinking about one colleague, a teacher who is there for only a semester's appointment. Nell says she started thinking about the other teacher's name tag, "like the plaque on her door," noticing that since the office is used by different temporary instructors each semester, "that name tag just . . . changes out." Nell surmises that her colleague is aware of her temporary status, and Nell wonders about making "this connection. . . what I'm trying to capture is like she's afraid of being interchangeable, like she wants to be special in some way." Nell tells us she wants to be able to build on this theme, saying she feels "a little bit of heat" or energy to fuel her writing there.

After Nell's introduction, we begin to read her revised poem. Like her original version, this poem begins with the excerpt of her journaling (which she did not revise from what appears in Chapter 3), where she contemplates the discomfort of being alone, the "crazy, irrational things" her colleagues do, and her fear that she might be able to "see myself 10 years from now." Nell's revised poem follows:

Older Single Women

It's dark but I
see her eyes take their
jagged journey around
the room. She squints in
the smoke,
stops,
still staring,
and elbows my abdomen.
"The tall one, at the bar. Green shirt."

I squint across our table,
above the heads of our friends,

through blue smoke
that makes my eyeliner burn.
I can't see him. "Yeah!
You should go up there.
Maybe he'll buy you a drink."
When she and I are
alone, it's martinis.
When we're with the guys,
it's India Pale Ale.
I shake my head apologetically
at our friends.
They're men, too,
but not tall, and not bald.
She likes them bald.
She takes a sip and leaves
her IPA at our table.

At school, her office plaque
is stamped with
"Instructor."
You can switch out the name card
if you shove it out of the track,
shove in another name
at the new semester.

I sip my drink and wonder
how she thinks love works.
Does she think she'll meet someone
in a bar,
stay up all night forging a connection
that will survive three time zones?
Is she willing to move back to [this state]?
At 37 and in Los Angeles,
she'd only be leaving a rental home
and a freelance writing job.
A wine and dinner club.
A handful of ex-boyfriends
and recently divorced maybes.

As we each finish reading, we are unanimous in liking Nell's revisions, and we eagerly point out favorite lines like "She likes them bald" and "I sip my drink and wonder/how she thinks love works." I then observe a shift from Nell's initial draft, where the focus was on the craziness, to this one where Nell is playing with a theme of impermanence. I wonder aloud about the woman who plays a central role: "What does she kind of want out of it? Like what is she going for here? Is she going for love, is she going for permanence, or is she going for maybe the exact opposite? And maybe that's why she chooses to be in a bar, prowling for men." This is an interesting development in the poem, as Nell links the "crazy" behavior she witnesses to an underlying fear of being replaceable.

This conversation brings us to explore Nell's own role as a character in her poem, and we wonder about how that relates to what she wants to accomplish with the writing. I comment, "The other thing that's really interesting in this is *you* . . . Like are you there just to observe her, or do you want . . . some of the reasons you are observing her to come out?" Karen says she had wondered the same thing, and Christina observes that the journaling at the beginning of the poem seems to beg this question. Christina explains that without the journaling, which is where Nell worries she might turn into these women in 10 years, Nell makes sense as just an observer. But if Nell keeps the journaling in the text, then Christina says as a reader she is "definitely gonna want to know whether you come to some sort of resolution in your head . . . or any conclusion in your thinking of the situation after observing her."

Through our questions about Nell's role in her own poem, we diverge from Nell's revisions and begin to talk about events and meaning that are not even present in her text. Nell laughs as she responds to our questions, saying she hopes to come across as "a more rational, more detached observer" in the poem, a contrast to these particular colleagues. She is never unkind as she discusses her poem or colleagues, again commenting, "I look at them and see myself 10 years from now." This makes her worry, "Oh my God! Like it only takes time, maybe?" Nell's lighthearted tone soon has us all laughing as she adds, "So the whole time I'm like watching and trying to say, 'no, I couldn't do that!' . . . So it's kind of this weird melding of observation . . . and also fear of myself, of what I'm capable of doing or incapable of doing." Nell's tongue-and-cheek concern for her own future is not present in the poem at all, and Nell tells us she had not intended to keep the journaling in her final version. So a significant layer of meaning, which drew her to write this poem and relates directly to how Nell sees herself, is located beyond the lines of her poem.

When I ask Nell to describe some of the crazy things she has observed, so we can better understand the worry she describes, she begins telling additional animated stories. We frequently punctuate Nell's storytelling with laughing commands to "write that down!" especially as her stories become more visual and as she describes some particularly outlandish antics. Nell responds to our laughter and enjoyment as she picks stories to tell and as she relays them. At some point Christina begins scribing as Nell talks, later posting her notes for Nell to use in future writing. Despite the role these stories play in Nell's thinking about this topic, however, they do not yet appear in her poem itself.

Across Nell's writing and our discussion of her text, she is creating more than just her poem. While we do spend a good deal of time discussing Nell's text (her revisions, our reactions, possibilities and questions for future versions), our discussions soon shift to Nell's role in the poem and the additional stories that inspired her writing. It is through these stories that Nell describes her fear of becoming like some of these other women, worrying that the longer she stays in that context, the greater the possibility that she might begin to display similar behaviors. As Nell writes about one woman's impermanence, and as she tells stories of what others do in their dating lives, she allows herself to also give voice to her own concerns, trying to figure out how she might be different from (or the same as) them. Here, while she is absolutely still developing her written text, she is also actively defining herself in important ways. She is using her poetry and journaling, as well as her oral questions, storytelling, self-descriptions (a "more rational, more detached observer"), and humorous comments to contrast herself with her colleagues and compose a separate identity for herself. This combination of strategies supports Nell in her ongoing creation of her own sense of self in her new home.

Playing with Genre: Karen's "Reflections of a First-Year Teacher"

Karen's experiences teaching 8th-grade English Language Arts in an urban school featured prominently in the journaling she shared during our previous meeting (see Chapter 3). Now, two weeks later, she describes new challenges her school is facing, including the resignation of several additional teachers. "I just found out that I'm getting seven new students because a language arts teacher is leaving us," she tells us during our reconnecting time. These new students will join her classes within the week, and more students may follow soon. "Teachers in my school are dropping like flies," she says. "Last week two more teachers quit." Karen attributes these resignations in part to the challenging teaching context, observing that students recently "made" a male teacher cry. She estimates that eight teachers have quit so far (a little over halfway into the year), contributing to a schoolwide lack of stability. She says her students even thought she had quit when she did not show up for school on the day that she had her teacher-of-the-year interview.

In addition to gaining new students in her own classes, Karen often has to cover other classes during her prep period. "That's a pain in the butt," she says, "because [then] I'm a substitute teacher." As we comment on how hard this must be to lose her prep period, Karen responds, "We don't really have prep periods anyway," because her free period is already taken up most days with required meetings. "So basically," she says, "I'm just giving up my meeting time." It now makes even more sense why Karen is at school past 6 o'clock each evening and why she had written about fears of failure in that earlier journaling.

Even in the midst of sharing these challenges, however, Karen is cracking jokes. When she remembers that I am recording our meeting, Karen exclaims, "I can't believe this is being taped! Christine, you have my life in your hands!" I offer to turn off the recorder, but Karen laughs my offer away. She seems well aware that having made it this far, she has outlasted many of her former colleagues. This exchange also points to a benefit of writing with colleagues who are outside one's own institution: Our writing group offers a safe space to vent and make sense of situations without the fear of word making it back to colleagues or supervisors.

When Karen introduces her writing, she tells us, "I just came up with a new idea for my writing today during school. And I think what I'm going to be working on now . . . is, um, a multi-genre piece about my first year teaching." She says she is "really excited about it" and worked on it just a bit that day, while her students took a test. She then directs us to her draft, a series of fictional emails she has written to parody high-pressure communications from various administrators. The first of these emails appears below:

To: Staff
From: Ms. X

Staff,

1. Please remember to be on duty at all times. If you stay in your room to speak with a student for even a minute while we are being audited, we LOSE points. Last time we lost several points. Let's not let that happen again.
2. How are your data notebooks coming? How is data driving instruction? Can you show evidence if someone asks to see your data notebook?
3. PEPs. We will be audited very soon.
4. IEPs, also expecting an audit in the near future.
5. Lesson plans MUST be submitted by Friday for the following week. Refer to the format sent in an earlier email. KEEP THESE ON THE CORNER OF YOUR DESK.
6. Please arrive to meetings ON TIME. Teams meet with Ms. J. on Mondays. Tuesday and Wednesday meeting with parents. Thursday meet with department. Friday meet with team and counselor. Cover student concerns.
7. You should be contacting parents of children with Ds and Fs on a regular basis.
8. Tardy policy. We will correct our tardy problem if we stick to the policy. NOTIFY parents when children are tardy. Send home tardy letters.
9. Please remember our staff meeting this Wednesday after school. We will have a data specialist here to discuss our numbers.
10. Submit a list of students who are struggling to me and grade-level counselor by Friday at 3.

Please remember, if your kids are not learning, you are not teaching.

Karen's decision to parody administrative emails allows her to exaggerate with comic effect the messages she and her colleagues often receive. She describes herself as "getting sick of emails" and describes her purpose as venting that frustration. Through her strategic use of genre, Karen is able to *show* the auditing, oversight, and micromanagement that drains her professionally.

After we read, Karen tells us she is starting to imagine other genres she could also include, such as "text boxes [with] things that I write on the board," narrative, and poetry. "Today I was thinking about how my board has changed over the course of the year," she explains. "In the beginning it was all rainbow-colored . . . because I had all these new Expo markers I'd bought." But she tells us "Over the course of the year all of my things have gotten stolen," which has led her boards to look quite different at this point. Karen says that while her board at one time may have said, "'Remember, today's a new day! Let's make this one great!" in multicolored ink, today her boards are more likely to remind students to raise their hands.

Karen also tells us she envisions writing little "in-between pieces" to track "all the teachers who quit." She imagines sprinkling a series of goodbyes to these departing teachers among the other texts in her envisioned collection: "like, Goodbye Johnson! Bye O'Donald! Peace out, Ms. Anderson!" Just as when Nell shared stories earlier, Karen *performs* her stories orally, playing to her audience and taking in our laughter as she suggests each new "goodbye." Christina observes, "I think this is going to be a really funny piece" and suggests ways to exaggerate moments in order to amplify that humor even more. This discussion also serves to further define Karen, who is clearly positioned as one of the teachers who is staying (and therefore in a position to bid others farewell).

We have no problem imagining the potential of Karen's plans. As Karen writes and plans this text, she deliberately uses her writing and storytelling to cope with the challenges she is facing as a new teacher. The odds are against her, and yet she identifies herself as someone who is sticking it out. As we laugh alongside Karen, therefore, it is with the shared recognition that comedy punctuates the serious, and that the humor is masking some difficult moments for Karen and her colleagues.

Nell observes, "The humor is great, but also the way it works is that then those really hard parts, if you even want to include them, then they can be more poignant in that way." I agree with Nell, observing that the contrast between the funny and the frustrating could work very well, and Christina asks Karen what genre she might use to help her incorporate these more serious moments. Karen says she might use poetry or a narrative blurb, "'cause I already have some things that I would like to put in there. But I don't want it to only, just like you guys were saying, I don't want it to only be funny. I want the parts that are crazy, like these emails, to maybe be funny, because they are so ridiculous. But like I just mostly want it to be . . .

I just want to remember this year." Karen is contemplative as she continues, "Because I want it to be over, but then I wanna . . . just remember it . . . So." She pauses a moment, thoughtful, and then continues, more upbeat, "I don't know, I'm sort of excited about this!"

Our conversation here has moved between Karen's posted text and her plans for future parts of that text. Much of our conversation has been humorous as we laugh about Karen's changing class boards (we each can see our own past idealism in those descriptions) and her joking "good-byes" to the teachers who have quit and whose students now crowd into Karen's own classroom. But Nell points out amid the laughter, there are really hard parts to Karen's experience as well, suggesting that the humor might provide a sort of comic relief and make those difficult moments even more poignant.

As the meeting continues, Nell asks Karen if she wants to include texts from students' perspectives as well, or if she wants it to just focus on her own point of view. Karen likes the idea, and Nell wonders if Karen might consider including confiscated student notes. Nell's question reminds Karen of "a funny comment" which she immediately says, "I need to write down." She goes on to tell us the story of a conversation with her students:

> I was telling [my students] this story about how these basketball players from like another team were like pushing my kids all over. And I was like, "I care about you guys so much . . . like when [that other team's player] was pushing you all over, like people had to hold me back . . . to not go talk to those boys!" And one of my boys was like, "What was you gonna do Ms. M? Shoot 'em with rainbows and smiles?"

Karen's retelling of this story is a performance of the moment, complete with reenacting her own teacher voice and her students' voices, and as her "audience" we are laughing out loud and telling her "yeah, that needs to go in there!" Our reaction leads Karen right into another story about how her students "basically say everything to my face." She tells us, "Today this one girl says to me, 'I just don't like you. I'm not ever going to like you. I just don't like you.' And I [basically said], 'That's fine, but you need to still be respectful in my class.'"

"What an incredible role model you showed her," I observe. "That 'no you don't have to like everybody, and it's okay if you don't like me.' I mean she is so immersed in being an 8th-grader . . . where they really do want everybody to like them, or to actively hate them. Like those are the two places of power."

"Yeah," Karen agrees. "I think she was really confused, because I was like . . . I don't care if you don't like me, I still like you. So, you're here to stay! But I think that . . . she really does want me to just care about her

. . . .And I do." When Karen finishes this story, I suggest that a dialogue or script of that exchange with her student could also be something she includes in her multi-genre piece. "Yeah, I could do that," she responds, "That would be cool."

This is already the most elaborate piece that Karen has brought to our group meetings, and certainly the first piece she is actively excited about revisiting. Whereas in our previous meeting, Karen had been resistant to writing nonfiction anymore and had described herself as "bad at revision," saying that when she writes something she then doesn't want to reenter it again, today she is excited to keep working on this piece.

Part of this energy may come from the fact that Karen is doing more than just writing a multi-genre text here. As she observes in her comments to us, she is also composing a way of remembering this incredible and challenging first year. Like Nell, Karen is an entertaining storyteller, with a natural sense of timing and humor. She easily has us laughing at all the right moments, as she parodies high-pressure emails and pokes fun at her own initial idealism. She uses this storytelling ability to gather ideas, and we mark writing opportunities with demands for her to "write down" ideas for later drafts. Christina even begins to scribe for Karen, to help her preserve this energy. Karen uses genre strategically to show the good and the bad, and these creative ideas fuel her energy for writing.

Across these conversations, Karen also can be seen composing a sense of herself as a teacher. By bidding departing teachers farewell, Karen defines herself as a teacher who is able to persevere, even when others do not. In her storytelling, as she plans future additions to her text, Karen also reveals herself as a teacher who cares for her students, who interacts personably and with humor in her classroom, and who is able to respond appropriately with reluctant students. As we discuss Karen's writing and stories, we also assist her in composing this professional identity, describing her as a role model and applauding her interactions with students.

Writing the Self as a Character:
Christina's Poem-Narrative "Identity Crisis Revisited"

Like Karen, Christina teaches in a challenging urban school context. As an English as a Second Language teacher and ESL program coordinator, Christina has struggled to find time for herself and her own life amid her many professional demands. These themes continue to surface in the extended version of "Identity Crisis" she shares in this meeting.

During our reconnecting time, Christina leads off with an animated story of being called down to the media center to claim some boxes, which turned out to be the textbooks she had ordered for her students. "It was a huge victory!" she exclaims, adding that the following day, after not being able to log onto or record grades or attendance on her school's computer program since December, she finally got that fixed. "And then Wednesday," she continues, "we got my high school students' schedules fixed, so they are actually in my class now, 5 weeks into the [second] semester." When we congratulate her on these obstacles falling away, Christina agrees, saying, "They are little victories, but they feel huge for me." Each story represents hours of work and frustration for her; it is no wonder that she had written herself as a solitary heroine in her epic poem.

When it is Christina's turn to share her writing, she tells us she's proud that she has been writing more often on her blog, and she also figured out how to import her past blog entries and her journal onto her current blog. "So now I have this complete collection of what I have been writing over the past 5 years." She then directs us where to find her text. When she left off last time, her character was standing alone, determined and immovable, facing a shadowy creature that salivated "at the scent of youth, of passion, of naivety." Her character was vulnerable, and her narrative that followed the poem revealed that Christina felt in danger of being consumed by the demands of her job. She wondered why she felt so willing to be a sacrifice, and thought that perhaps her own ambition was the creature she was fighting. Today, Christina directs us to skip past what we read last time and begin with the next installment, where she finally engages the creature in battle and draws first blood:

Identity Crisis Revisited

I raise my sword to my adversary,
Meeting those dark red eyes with my own,
Hoping to convey stalwartness and determination
And to hide my doubts and fears behind my blade.
The creature lunges toward me—the battle has begun—
Its warm breath fills my nostrils as I leap away,
It is strong and vigorous, bemused by my facade.
The tremendous head quivers from side to side,
Toying with me as I leap back and forth,
Seeming to smirk at my hesitation.
Enraged, I leap forward, driving my weapon forward.
The metal slices through dark matted hair and leathery skin.
[NOTE: something about raw...meat...]
As I wrench my weapon out,
I am torn by my first taste of victory
And the consuming fear of failure.

Small victories. That's what keeps me going through the day-to-day hoops that I have to jump through. Case in point: Monday morning was like Christmas—a highly unusual feeling for any teacher, let alone a first-year teacher who is plagued by the constant worry that she is behind. I was in the copy room, hoping that I had enough paper to make handouts for the first half of the day, cursing the [lack of supplies]. ...Yes, we went a whole week without paper. And had to start the next week without supplies. Time to break out the stone and chisel . . .

As I pleaded with the copier to miraculously produce a sufficient amount of handouts, a fellow teacher walked in, announcing, "Hey, you have a bunch of boxes in the media center."

Boxes? I wonder what it could be.

Grabbing my copies, I nearly ran down through our labyrinth of a school, down three sets of stairs and two hallways into the other building where the media center is housed. Flinging open the door, my hands went to my face in amazement. My books!

This small victory was the result of months of developing my curriculum, researching a variety of textbooks, writing a proposal and presenting my work to the school board. Six months into the school year and I now had textbooks to teach with, a large step to legitimizing my classroom and what I was teaching on a daily basis. No longer did I have to make every single handout . . . for my class. My students had *books*.

Not surprisingly, the "small victories" Christina had shared at the beginning of our meeting figure prominently in this next layer of her piece. Our discussion reveals how very much "like Christmas" this must have been—receiving her books meant no more copying and worrying about paper shortage or copier malfunction. It has been an epic battle, and Christina depicts herself emerging, for now, victorious. Perhaps it is this sense of triumph that shifts the standoff between Christina and the creature.

Christina writes herself into each of these texts, allowing her to develop her own identity through these two genres. In the poem, Christina depicts herself as the hero warrior, armed for battle with her sword raised against this creature. She crafts her character as brave in the face of her own fears, agile enough to stay just beyond the creature's reach, and strong enough to drive her sword into the creature's tough hide. She also acknowledges her own vulnerability, showing herself constructing a deliberate facade of "stalwartness and determination" in hopes of hiding her fears. While it is her adversary's smirk that ultimately enrages her into action, Christina ends this section of the poem by acknowledging her "consuming fear of failure."

In her corresponding narrative, Christina links her "first taste of victory" with "legitimizing my classroom and what I was teaching on a daily basis." Even in this text, Christina uses language that invokes an epic-scale battle, as she writes herself running through a "labyrinth" of a school, facing the school board with a proposal, and ultimately providing for her students. Thus, in both the poem and the narrative, Christina is using writing to help her compose an identity as a teacher, showing herself as prevailing, even just for the moment, on behalf of her students.

As we finish reading, our conversation returns to a topic from our previous meeting, and we talk about what the creature might represent. "Now, the creature, the creature is the fear?" I ask.

"I still haven't decided what the creature is," Christina replies. "That was something that I was kind of playing with before . . . I haven't decided if the creature is going to be like you're saying, my fear or my fear of failure . . . so the creature ends up being myself. Or if the creature is going to be the school, which is originally how I imagined it." She laughs a little uncomfortably. "I haven't clarified it enough in my head to even say it to you."

I comment that sometimes writing and talk work that way, where it is hard to find the words we need when we are not sure quite what we want to express. "Try to talk about it just around the edges of it then," I suggest.

"So, basically what I'm getting at," Christina begins again, "the things I'm dealing with in my writing, and that I'm sort of working through—*through* my writing—is this idea of . . . what am I really planning on doing. The question has come up because I'm trying to figure out what things are going to look like for me next year. I have the opportunity to potentially move to a different school district." She trails off a bit as she says this, and then continues. "What that means for me in my head is do I move to a different school . . . and then my life would end up being easier. I wouldn't have quite so many obstacles at the [new] district I would be at. Um, or do I want to sort of continue to work through what I'm doing here. And so in that sense that is what I mean. . . . Is the creature the school or is the creature myself because I am the one sort of self-imposing. . . ." Again, Christina's volume trails off as she finishes.

"Yeah, that makes a lot of sense," I reply, and then ask, "I don't remember if you ask it specifically, but *why* are you in it?" As I continue, I try to articulate some possible reasons Christina might have for staying in her current district: "Is it making a change in a school? Is that it? So that is sort of like a programmatic change. Is it staying on in the lives of certain kids? Is it sustaining and growing as a teacher? With the expectation that there are lots of different kids that you will come in contact with over your career?" Overall, I suggest that perhaps Christina is trying to "figure out a way to sustain yourself, so that . . . you live to fight another day." I laugh here at my attempt to pick up on Christina's metaphor.

"Right," Christina responds. "You are exactly getting at what I'm struggling with here."

"Yeah, that's part of what I think can be really tricky . . . my guess is that quite possibly this creature is all of these things," I say.

"Mmmmm," says Christina. "Yeah. I would agree with that."

Throughout this conversation, we are once again composing meaning *beyond* the text as we explore the identity of the creature and its relation to Christina and her pending career decisions. Christina is trying to figure out whether she can continue to be a teacher in her current school, or if she will try to seek a different opportunity. Once again, this involves significant identity work for her. What are her priorities as a teacher and person, at this point in her life? What are her fears? The creature is a significant part of the epic poem, and its identity remains shadowy for good reason, because Christina is still actively figuring out what it represents.

When I suggest that Christina does not need to understand all the significance of her own writing before discussing it, I encourage her to compose meaning as she talks. It is at this point that Christina begins to articulate the possibility of changing jobs, and she acknowledges using her writing to work through this decision. Rather than writing about this decision overtly, perhaps listing the pros and cons of staying or leaving, Christina writes herself as a character in an epic battle, the outcome of which she is unsure, but which seems tied to whether she will stay at her school.

"I really love the images in this metaphor," Nell adds, returning us to our discussion about the creature's identity. As Nell tries to orally work out what she is trying to say, she initially sounds uncertain, yet as she continues her voice becomes louder, faster, and filled with increased conviction:

> I think that part of the beauty is that it's indefinable in some ways
> . . . I guess sometimes in writing . . . we do need to know what it is
> . . . But I think the nature of this, like fear, like when you have fear, or
> when you are doing something new or struggling with some issue. . . .
> We rarely have all the pieces there, and you still have to make your decision anyway, whether to fight or to run or whatever. And so, I think
> part of the beauty is, for me, right now, is that it's . . . kind of ambiguous. Because that's almost—in a way, it's almost inconsequential.

Here Nell is trying to articulate something slippery, an awareness that Christina hinted at earlier. While this is a piece of writing that we are discussing, the content of the writing is not formed or even completely known to the writer. Rather, Christina is moving between genres here as she seeks to define something that seems to still elude her. And Nell is encouraging her to allow herself to keep things ambiguous, to not feel compelled to define the creature or to seek a neat resolution.

As we finish talking about Christina's piece, I ask Karen, who has been quiet through much of the conversation, if she has anything to add. "No, not at this time," she responds, laughing, "I really am enjoying it though, and I think it's a great metaphor . . . I feel really selfish when I read your things, Christina, because I'm always like, 'oh my gosh, I feel the same thing!'"

Just as with the other examples in this chapter, it is clear that Christina is composing beyond her written texts. Even as she adds this whole new installment of her story, she also ties in her own real-life accomplishments and decision making. In doing so, through writing and talk Christina composes overlapping identities as a new teacher who is at once strong and vulnerable, brave and fearful. By allowing herself to write in a less conventional genre and style, Christina allows herself to write about ideas that are still unformed while exploring how she feels in relation to these forces. She also gives her own unease a figure in her poem, casting herself as a hero in an epic battle with this creature. In doing so, Christina crafts an identity for herself as a teacher who is ultimately resilient and strong, even as she works in demanding circumstances.

Christina also uses her writing to help understand a problem and work toward a decision regarding her next career steps. In our discussion Nell observes that as much as we might discuss the identity of the creature, in life we often must act even when we do not have "all the pieces." Nell reframes this ambiguity as part of the value of Christina's text, saying in some ways the creature's identity is "inconsequential," that Christina will still have to make a decision even if she does not know what the creature fully represents. This reframing gives Christina permission to not know all the answers, to not know what causes her discomfort exactly, but to see that she can still make a decision anyway.

Across the three examples in this chapter, we can see teacher-writers developing meaningful texts in partnership with writing group members. They are also creating more than just those textual artifacts. In writing and talk, they compose identities as teachers, survivors, warriors, friends, women, and role models. They also create ways of socializing, remembering, persevering, and making decisions, even in the midst of their challenging first years as teachers.

Suggestions and Guiding Questions for Composing Identities and Ways of Being

Consider Your Role in Your Writing

- Are you a character in your own piece of writing? If so, how do you want to depict yourself?
- How does the way you depict yourself relate to your purpose for writing? Are there opportunities to reimagine your self-depiction so that it more closely aligns with your purpose?
- Compare yourself to other characters or individuals featured in your text. What does your interaction with these other characters reveal about you? About them?

Play with Genre

- Free yourself to consider other genres for your writing. How might poetry or fiction, or even a less conventional genre like an email or a list, help you explore your topic and thinking from a different angle?
- Is there an opportunity to shift genre within a piece of writing, or deliberately use multiple genres to write about different aspects of your overall topic?
- How can you use genre to help you imagine other possibilities or ways of seeing your topic? Do alternate genres allow you to ignore constraints related to reality or time?
- Can writing through a different genre allow you to better *show* something to your readers, even if you are still working on articulating it for yourself?
- How might humor play a role in what you write?

Invest in Discussion and Oral Storytelling

- Talk through stories that relate to your topic. Pay attention to the energy and reactions of your audience to help identify what else you can include in your writing.
- Ask a group member to act as a scribe for you, to help you capture key elements of your oral storytelling.
- As soon as possible after telling stories and discussing your ideas, make time to write so you can take advantage of some of the energy that is generated.
- Resist limiting yourself on what or when to share. You don't have to know all the answers before you talk about an idea or text.
- Write and talk through decisions, even when you are most unsure of where a text or a topic is going. Play with language, try out possible meanings, and experiment.

Follow Your Energy and Respect Your Experience While Writing

- Respect your own energy as you write. Try to identify when you feel most excited or drawn to continue writing, and try to nurture that energy.
- Observe your experiences across your composing processes—not just the writing, but the talk and thinking about that writing as well. Build on energy that you observe, and make time to write about those topics or ideas that you find yourself most excited to discuss.
- Respect that some texts do not need to be finished or shared publicly in order to be significant. Your experience while writing a text may be significant and transformative in itself.

CHAPTER 8

"A More Complicated Human Being"
Inventing Teacher-Writers

What does it mean to be a writer? I think it comes down to the essential nature of writing. Writing is something that you *do*, not something that you *know*, and when you think about it that is an incredibly important understanding for us to have as teachers of writing.

—Katie Wood Ray, *The Writing Workshop: Working through the Hard Parts*
(And They're All Hard Parts) (2001, italics in original)

It was also a nice chance to shift and think about myself as a writer, but to also think about myself as ... a more complicated human being than just a teacher.

—Karen, reflecting on our writing group experience

"I remember the first time I came," Jillian reminisces, a year after we began meeting. "I kind of was thinking I had to have almost a finished piece [of writing]." She laughs briefly at the memory. "And I only had a little section, and I was like, 'okay, here's a poem I think?' And I felt kind of, you know, self-conscious. That I didn't have this *great* grand piece. But just the fact that, you know, I got support from the group and feedback of what they liked . . . what *you* liked about it, and directions I could take it. I mean that was *huge*."

Having people enjoy our writing and receiving generative feedback, even about small pieces or ideas for future writing, has propelled each of us to write more and try new things as writers. Across our first year as a writing group, we each learned to bring our writing at all stages to group meetings, and we shared a range of personal and professional texts, written for a variety of audiences. In the process, we composed texts we are proud of and used our writing to explore and shape our ways of being in the world.

As we reflect on our first year together, during the same writing group meeting that opens this book, Christina adds, "I think . . . even though as first-year teachers, carving out this extra time to be a part of the group could initially seem daunting, I think it was a really healthy move for us. It gave us each a way to connect with each other. It gave us a way to talk to each other at critical moments. And like [Karen] said, it helped you to affirm that you are more than a teacher."

Christina's words, which echo Karen's observations about the value of thinking of herself as a "more complicated human being," have continued to resonate with each of us in our writing group. Teaching can loom large in our lives, sometimes casting other complex ways of being into shadow, as we find ourselves planning lessons while in line at the grocery store or thinking about a student while having coffee with friends. Having the opportunity and support to focus on being writers, and through writing to explore our interests within and beyond the walls of our classrooms, has indeed felt healthy.

Christina's and Karen's comments also help foreground teacher-writers as whole people. Much of the literature on teachers as writers tends to emphasize our *teacher* roles, often depicting writing in service to our students and profession, either on the local classroom level or the larger educational landscape. The explicit intention of much of this literature is to encourage teachers' writing for just these reasons, recognizing that when we write we are better able to shape instruction from the inside, as a fellow writer in the classroom. Yet these are just some of the benefits that teacher-writers can experience. The examples in this book show us, as teacher-writers, creating space for writing, finding inspiration amid our everyday lives, nurturing ideas in our heads and on paper, and building cohesion across our writing lives.

This final chapter looks across the preceding chapters, in an effort to synthesize strategies and outcomes, as well as begin to look beyond this first year in a writing group. We formed our group based on our interests and goals, and we adapted our choices based on our unfolding experiences. My hope is that you, as a teacher interested in writing, may adapt and combine strategies from across this book to fit your own needs and priorities. The goal is not to reproduce our writing group in other contexts, which may not honor the individuality of our writing group members or of other teacher-writers. Rather, I hope you will feel empowered to craft your own commitments, routines, and practices, as you seek to create a supportive and generative writing community.

CREATING A SUSTAINABLE WRITING GROUP—IN PERSON OR ONLINE

I began Chapter 2 with an excerpt of Judy Brown's (2006) poem "Fire," which reminds us, "What makes a fire burn/ is space between the logs;" piling on too many logs can put out a fire as "surely as a pail of water." Within the pages of this book, I have tried to show that writing may be experienced as the space between the logs, a "breathing space" we can create and protect amid those other things that both fuel and sometimes smother our fires.

Each member of the writing group helps create space, for the self and for others. By engaging in discussions, shaping group commitments, sharing writing, and providing feedback on others' texts, each member helps articulate practices that other members may then adapt and use. Creating space is a collaborative process, and support matters. The following strategies and themes run across the preceding chapters of this book.

Articulate Shared Commitments

In seeking to create space for writing, our writing group found it critical to articulate our priorities about what types of writing we wanted to do, as well as what we hoped to experience *during* meetings. These conversations helped us prioritize feeding our "fires" as writers.

As you contemplate beginning a writing group, consider your priorities. Part of what will draw you and other members back to your writing group will be the experience you have while you are there. What will make you enjoy meeting together? How much planning or organization do your particular members need in order to feel productive and also comfortable? Keeping our writing group routines simple, yet flexible, has worked well for us. We value our reconnecting time, as it allows us to prioritize our relationships with each other and build on our foundation of trust. And we value ensuring that each member has time to talk about writing during each meeting, even if all someone brings is an idea for future writing.

In our own writing group, we spent early meetings experimenting, trying various technologies and playing with different structures and routines. We are flexible even now, as we sometimes decide to write together during a meeting if no one has brought a text, or as we share resources and writing ideas we glean from other sources. In the past several years, we have tried other strategies, such as reading a shared book about writing or engaging in a joint inquiry into a particular genre. For example, one month we all decided to work on humor writing, reading mentor texts and even inviting a local guest author to join us for a writing group meeting.

In our group, we prioritize *doing writing* on a regular basis, which requires us to commit ourselves to flexibility and choice. Because we want to *write* for ourselves with enjoyment, we often emphasize our processes and practices as writers over our production of texts. So we choose what we share, how we share it, at what stage we bring writing, and even if we share at all. As authors, we also choose what happens to our own texts. Sometimes we spend a great deal of time on a text, taking it through many revisions, and sometimes we set a text aside for a while to follow our energy and write something else. Protecting this range of choices may seem counterintuitive, especially if you are seeking an incentive to write and develop specific texts, yet it has been a critical element of our particular group's flexibility and success. From the start, we did not want to feel the need to apologize or feel guilty if we did not bring writing to share. Just coming to meetings to talk about other group members' writing allows us to build writing practices and ideas for the future. For us, the most important goals are to keep participating and keep writing.

With that said, there have been moments over the past several years when each of us has had to step back and miss several meetings in a row. Significant life events, work conflicts, and other obstacles have interfered at times for each of us. When these situations arise, our approach has been to make sure that every member continues to feel welcome, and to reach out to each other outside of writing group meetings. In this way, we continue to connect with each other, sometimes even just individually, until the member is able to once again participate in meetings.

We have designed a writing group experience that focuses on supporting writing that matters to us, rather than an experience that focuses on how our writing can shape our teaching. This decision does set us apart from other teacher writing groups. Aside from our reconnecting time, we spend the rest of our meetings discussing our writing, giving full attention to what each writer wants, without then feeling obligated to analyze our moves or how we could use these experiences to inform our teaching. In many ways this has been a freeing decision for our members, so that we can deliberately foreground ourselves as whole people and explore topics for writing freely. When ideas for our teaching come up organically, we talk about them, but we do not typically dedicate meeting time to discussing our teaching.

Take the Writing Group Online!

After articulating goals for your writing group experience, it is easier to begin to define routines and logistics. Many of the practices shared in this book would work as well for an in-person writing group as they do for our online meetings. In our case, we were geographically dispersed, so we faced a challenge of how to create the experience we envisioned in an online setting. While we could have focused primarily on textual response, with group members electronically exchanging writing and then receiving only written feedback on the texts, such an asynchronous approach would not have allowed for the rich conversations and expanded ways of participating that our group was seeking.

It did not take long for us to realize that our online necessity may have offered us one of our greatest opportunities as a writing group. Because we meet exclusively online, our group has been able to maintain a sense of flexibility and responsiveness, which has allowed each of us to continue participating. From the start, Karen and Nell lived too far away to drive to an in-person meeting, and within the first year I, too, moved out of state. For a face-to-face writing group, each of us would have been cut off once we were too far to drive comfortably. Because we just need a computer and an Internet connection to gather, however, we have been able to set meetings to fit everyone's schedule. Nell was even able to continue participating when she took a fellowship opportunity in China one year; we just had to do some creative time zone adjustments to make sure we could find a common meeting time.

For our actual meetings we most commonly use Skype or Google Hangout, and we try to use video conferencing if possible. It is really nice to be able to see each other as we meet, but sometimes members' poor Internet connections or computer issues require us to go back to audio-only conference calls. We use text messaging and the chat feature on our conference call to supplement our communication, letting each other know if we are running late or need to briefly step away from our computers. We also use these features to quickly share websites, music, video, or other texts that may be relevant for our conversations. In this way members can find and share resources that may relate to our writing, perhaps in content or as a mentor text. Over the years, we have expanded our ways of sharing writing as well. The most important thing for us has been trial and error, trying a new technology when someone hears about it or uses it elsewhere and collaboratively deciding how to adapt our usage to our needs and priorities.

CREATING SUSTAINABLE WRITING PRACTICES

As the previous chapters have highlighted, our writing group drew on a number of strategies to help us compose texts and writing practices. These strategies include discussing what we do and experience as writers, considering audience and purpose, foregrounding talk and relationships, expanding what we count as writing, and making connections across our writing lives. These strategies may be readily adapted and combined by other teacher-writers, as you seek to craft your own writing practices and writing group experiences.

Notice and Name Writing Opportunities and Strategies

There truly can be writing opportunities all around us. In our writing group, we try to stay open to writing opportunities by noticing and acting on ideas, even in a quick piece of writing. The more regularly we write, and the more we anticipate and think about our writing, the more readily we begin to find inspiration for writing all around us. Jillian noticed the feeling she had when reading a student's note, I observed the poetry in my aunt's email language, and Karen imagined writing a quick parody of an administrator's email. In each of these cases, we not only shared the texts that we wrote as a result of a triggering idea, but we also shared our ways of finding ideas. As a result of our writing group meetings, I now look at notes and emails in a different light, because I have seen writing emerge from them.

Even the ways we "do" writing are worth discussing. In Chapter 3, Nell shared her quandary over whether to handwrite or type, as well as how these physical acts shape her experience composing and her ability to share her work. Technology can offer additional opportunities, such as Christina's use of a blog and Twitter to collect and develop writing ideas. As you work with your own writing partners, discuss your experiences with different ways of writing.

We also embrace sharing writing across all stages of a text, and in this way we seize opportunities, even if is just the 20 minutes before a meeting or during a lunch break. The writing we accomplish in these found moments can be just enough to share and spark future writing. Once again, we share not only the writing, but our ways of doing it. We discuss when and where we write, which helps other members begin to see opportunities and ways of writing. And we share and name some of the writing techniques we use, so that our own texts can become models for each other. Thus, as we talk about the specific things we admire in each other's texts, we are noticing techniques for strong writing that we can try in our own work. And as we question each other and are questioned about our writing, we expand what we might try in current and future projects. Peter Johnston (2004) reminds us that noticing and naming are "crucial to becoming capable in particular activities," and "once we start noticing certain things, it is difficult not to notice them again" (p. 11). As you invest in your own writing group experience, try to include time to talk about what you are doing as writers, to notice and name your strategies, so that you can collaboratively expand your sense of what is possible.

Acknowledge and Articulate Constraints

Like other writers and other teacher-writers, the members of our group face obstacles that sometimes threaten to block our writing. Sometimes the audience or context presents an obstacle to our writing. In those cases, discussing the interests and purposes of the audience, features of the genre, or aspects of the rhetorical situation can help us find ways to begin or redirect a piece of writing. Discerning the limitations and the expectations of particular writing tasks can help writers feel less constrained, often enabling us to figure out ways to adjust boundaries to fit our own needs or interests.

We are busy people, and limited time and energy also pose significant constraints to our writing. In our writing group, we have found it useful to acknowledge and articulate the challenges we face in order to create ways to overcome them. Our reconnecting time plays a key role in this process, as we talk about our busy schedules, the demands on us in our jobs and home lives, our energy levels, and how we are feeling in general. These are not simple therapy sessions; rather, we listen and respond, as friends and colleagues, about what is blocking us. We also discuss where we feel more free and energized. Acknowledging that constraints exist and are difficult to overcome can be an empowering move. It can be tempting to be hard on ourselves when we have difficulty as writers. In your own writing group, talk through your challenges together. Acknowledge these life situations as constraints and address them explicitly, so you might help each other create space for writing.

Sometimes the constraints we experience have less to do with external pressure and more to do with our own energy for a piece of writing. Our interests and life experiences may sometimes call us to write about some topics and may block us from writing about others. We have tried to respect and discuss our energy as writers. When Nell did not want to work on her poem about loneliness anymore after starting to date someone, or Karen did not want to write about teaching anymore because she needed a change, or I did not want to work on my found poem for my aunt because it made me sad, we experienced limitations as writers. Rather than looking at these moments of avoidance as problems to be overcome, we allow ourselves to set pieces of writing aside and follow our energy into a new piece of writing. Often we make our way back, when our energy shifts again. Of course, sometimes we have to persevere, especially if a text is required in a professional or academic context. Even then, talking about our energy and articulating what feels constraining is a useful strategy for getting "unstuck" and moving forward.

Talk in Varied Ways About Writing

Engaging in a talk-based writing group is a good way to foreground writing practices and relationships with other writers. Prioritizing our reconnecting time offers us opportunities to build community and trust with each other, which in turn supports our willingness to share deeply personal texts. Our writing group conversations include a variety of types of talk, which may be equally useful for other teacher-writers, as you tell stories, question texts and each other, and orally play with language possibilities.

Storytelling can be a powerful composing strategy, particularly when it is tied to even a beginning draft of a written text. In our group, we often tell stories to provide background information or context for a text, describe our audience or purpose, or even extend beyond what we have written to explore related themes. Often these stories help us generate content and take on a decidedly performative quality; in these moments we often tell each other to "write that down!" or find it useful for another member to scribe, to help preserve language that may be useful later.

One way to begin to generate useful stories among group members is to ask questions. For example, it was not until Christina asked me why my aunt is so significant to me that I began to tell stories of our experiences together. We ask genuinely curious questions, rooted in a respect for the author's expertise about her topic and text. We ask questions to help us understand (and help the author articulate) the audience, context, and overall purpose of a text. We inquire to clarify moments and encourage an author to expand on the significance of details in a text.

It is also critical that authors pose their own questions. In our writing group, we often ask group members to read our texts with certain things in mind, helping ensure that the feedback is focused on the author's needs. Authors also ask questions throughout the discussion of a text, to follow up on and clarify some of the feedback we receive. As we inquire, we often experiment with new language, rehearsing possible revisions that might respond to group feedback. As you work with your own writing group members, consider the role of storytelling and inquiry as you reconnect and as you explore your writing together.

Experiment with Genre and Technique

Playing with genre also can open up writing opportunities, in some cases creating energy for a text or expanding ways of representing a topic. For example, when Karen first shared journals about her teaching, she told us she wanted help finding a new genre, and she was considering writing fiction to give herself a mental break from the challenges of her job. When she then shifted to a multi-genre text to explore her first year of teaching, rather than writing *about* her frustration when receiving high-pressure emails from administrators, she actually composed parodies of those emails. Her use of exaggeration and humor allowed her to imagine several other genres that she could include in her piece. Similarly, Christina used poetry mixed with narrative to explore her first year of teaching, allowing her to represent her struggle through a metaphorical battle between herself and a shadowy creature. Nell's approach to her wedding toast offers another example, this time of Nell's purposeful switch from a speech-toast to a poem-toast, through which she was able to reimagine a difficult text in a more familiar genre. In all of these cases, the writers use genre strategically to help them gain traction and energy for writing.

Experimenting with genre also can help us explore our identities and ways of being in the world. By writing oneself as a particular type of character in a story or narrative, a writer can deliberately highlight or obscure certain aspects of reality. When Christina positioned herself as a solitary fighter, embroiled in a battle with a faceless creature, she was able to invent a sort of identity for herself in related situations. Even the decision to not place oneself into a text, to keep it distant or more formal, can have interesting results. In some ways, trying out different genres encourages us as writers to follow the maxim of "show, don't tell," enabling us to bring our readers more directly into an experience we hope to create. As you write and talk with other writers, consider how you might play with genre to foster energy and create opportunities.

There is a playfulness associated with this experimentation with genre and technique. There are wonderful resources available for writing teachers, with techniques and exercises designed to help us shape instruction and inspire our student writers (e.g., Atwell, 1998; Bomer, 2005; Dunning & Stafford, 1992; Fletcher & Portalupi, 2001; Heard, 1989; Hicks, 2013; Kittle, 2008; Ray, 2006). Consider mining these resources for writing exercises to share with your writing group as well. Similarly, there are inspiring guides designed for writers, which groups can explore in a shared study (e.g., Elbow, 1998; Goldberg, 2005; Heard, 1995; Lamott, 1995; Murray, 1996). Even if you just partner with another member of your writing group to play with techniques you find in outside resources, bring what works back to the full group for discussion and reflection.

Expand What Counts as Writing

In our writing group, we write and share a variety of texts, ranging from fully developed drafts to lists, outlines, character sketches, questions, journals, timelines, and freewrites. We share texts that we initiate, which are personal and may align with notions of "creative writing." We also write and share texts that we do not initiate, which we may feel compelled to write. In recognizing and sharing these varied types of writing in our meetings, we mobilize strategies for invention across contexts, and we include many more genres in what we count as "writing."

Expanding what counts as writing frees us to explore genre and follow our interests more broadly. It demystifies writing to some degree, allowing us to bring pieces that are still emerging. It also helps us use strategies across our personal and professional writing lives. In the literature on teachers as writers, work-related texts are often downplayed when teachers are encouraged to write. What our teacher writing group does, therefore, is explore ways that even job-related writing is worthy of attention, especially when we are able to mobilize writing strategies across personal and professional texts. As researcher Anne Elrod Whitney (2009) observes, a teacher's writing is "never neatly divided into personal or professional" (p. 253), but rather these strands are complex and often intertwine. Whitney encourages support for teachers to engage in both personal and professional writing, and to explore the purposes for each and the relationships between them.

Strategies like playing with style, writing about the professional in multiple (and not always traditional) genres, and analyzing a rhetorical situation in order to discover opportunities to manipulate genre can be seen as expanding what we consider as teacher writing. As you collaborate with other teacher-writers, consider ways to deliberately welcome and share a wide range of texts in writing group meetings, enabling you to observe and discuss varied ways of mobilizing familiar techniques. In doing so, you may find it easier to foreground your *ways of writing* and build cohesion in your writing lives.

FOREGROUNDING TEACHER-WRITERS' CREATIVITY

Across the chapters of this book, I have emphasized the significance of teachers' writing on its own terms, beyond whatever written texts or classroom benefits may also emerge. I focus on the creativity that teacher-writers display as we pursue our own writing, for our own purposes, in partnership with each other. This is not to say that other lines of inquiry, which consider how teachers' writing relates to their pedagogies or participation in the field, are not fruitful or needed. Instead, this book looks beyond those benefits to also consider how we craft ways of being writers, and how we may be shaped by our experiences writing together.

I hope this book has fostered inquiry into the possibilities associated with foregrounding creativity and play in teachers' writing lives. Across the social interactions presented in this book, as teacher-writers we endeavor to "do writing" in varied ways. We acknowledge the writing that weaves through our lives, and we create opportunities to pursue writing that has personal meaning. We endeavor to build cohesion, to use strategies across personal and professional texts, and to draw on our writing techniques to help us shape in-person interactions. In doing so, we compose not only texts but identities and ways of being writers and people in the world.

This book presents an extended view into our first year as a writing group, in an effort to spotlight how we got started and what we were able to create across that formative year. Currently, our writing group is preparing to begin our 8th year together, and we are still going strong. We continue to share a broad range of writing, emphasizing personal and self-initiated texts, but also including space for professional and academic writing. We keep trying new things, including collaboratively writing and presenting on our work together. Across our interactions, we continue to emphasize what we do as writers, taking notice of our writing strategies, discussing our energy and challenges, and seeking to participate regularly in writing group meetings.

In foregrounding our identities as *writers*, showing teachers as whole, "complicated" people, I hope to expand discussions about teachers as writers. We are siblings and parents, spouses and partners, friends and nieces. We dance and we coach, we read fantasy books and travel abroad, we live in cities and in small towns, we garden and tweet and send text messages. And we teach. Amid all of these other things we do and all of these people we are, we build relationships with our students, write lesson plans, grade student work, make bulletin boards, serve hall duty, and teach classrooms full of talented young people. We are teachers who value teaching, who want our students to see themselves as writers, and who think a great deal about our students and our pedagogy. We also *write*. In our writing group, and in our own time, we create space for writing and engage in acts of writing. Thus we are complex, teaching and more-than-teaching people, who savor success and fear failure, who can find poetry amid the little moments in life, and who can find truth and meaning among the lines of each other's poems.

Table of All Written Texts Shared During Focal Year

Texts that were initiated or assigned by someone other than the author are *italicized*. Texts that have professional or academic purpose/audience are also <u>underlined</u>.

	Christine	Christina	Nell	Jillian	Karen
12/4	Poem on fantasy books	Mother timeline		Pregnancy timeline	
12/11	Poem on fantasy books	School poem			
12/27	Christmas poem			"Dancing Game" narrative	Rant poem
1/15		"Foreign" (school poem)	"Comfortable Hell" poem	"Dancing Game"	
1/29	Poem on fantasy books			"Dancing Game"	
2/12	Letter to Angela	"Identity Crisis" poem/narrative	"Older Single Women" poem	"Dancing Game"	Journals about teaching
2/26	*Teaching award essay*	"Identity Crisis" poem/narrative	"Older Single Women"		Multigenre on teaching
3/26				Writing from student note	Multigenre on teaching

	Christine	Christina	Nell	Jillian	Karen
4/30	Journal ideas for writing about moving	"The Battle" (formerly "Identity Crisis")	*Wedding toast for sister (poem)*		
5/28	*Home information sheet*	*Presentation notes for Title III meeting*	*Wedding toast poem*	*Girl Quest article*	
6/25	Journal writing about home/moving		*Research design assignment for graduate class*		"The Luckiest" poem
8/6	List of found language from aunt's emails	"Barriers" vignettes	Found poem on lost text messages		
8/27	Gardening essay		*Life lessons essay*	Jo's rant—character sketch	
9/10	Oral brainstorming for essay			Oral brainstorming for fiction	
9/24		*School newsletter*			
10/22	Found poem for my aunt	*Introduction for grandmother's cookbook*	*Student recommendation letter*		

Studying Our Writing Group

It is fitting that acts of writing run throughout my study of this writing group, just as they do our writing group meetings. I wrote to transcribe audiorecordings, to annotate and reflect on transcripts and shared texts, and to compose (and revise and compose again) the stories and discussions I set forth in these chapters. Writing also runs throughout the ethnographic and narrative inquiry research traditions that inform this study (Clandinin & Connelly, 2000; Emerson et al., 1995; Heath & Street, 2008; Schaafsma & Vinz, 2011).

GATHERING TALK AND TEXTS

While our group continues to meet today, this book represents only the first thirteen months of our work together as a writing group, beginning in October 2008 and extending through November 2009. I focused on this particular time window to capture meetings for at least one calendar year (a full academic year plus the summer break), during which I could observe many instances of invention, including the collaborative creation of our writing group itself. I also wanted to provide a view into the early stages of our group, which I hoped would allow other teacher-writers to see how a writing group might start up, and what they might accomplish during their first year together. Extending my study through November 2009 allowed me to also include discussions from our two November 2009 meetings, during which we reflected on our first year together while planning for a national conference presentation.

Because my focus is on our writing group, and the ways we composed and shared our writing within that group, I gathered texts and talk shared during the focal 13 months of the study. In all, group members shared a total of 31 distinct texts, many of which involved several drafts. (Appendix A lists all written work that was shared during the focal year of this project). I recorded the social interactions during writing group meetings by taking fieldnotes and, after the first three months, audiorecording our meetings. Audiorecording the meetings allowed me to look more closely at our talk, providing a record of the stories that were told and the invention of texts and strategies for writing. I waited to begin audiorecording until February in order to allow the group time to get comfortable with the online technology. My fieldnotes functioned to preserve some of the contextual information about meetings (e.g., who attended and when they joined the meeting, technology issues, related emails or text messages, changes in routine), as well as to note primary themes that were discussed, texts that were shared, and reflections or thoughts I had during meetings. At the end of each fieldnote entry, I noted how the meeting concluded and who planned on attending the following meeting. In all, I had data for 20 writing group meetings, each 2 hours in length. I also had email correspondence and fieldnotes from several phone conversations with members between meetings.

ORGANIZING AND ANALYZING OUR TALK AND TEXTS

Writing fieldnotes and transcribing audiorecordings are, in themselves, interpretive acts (Emerson et al., 1995). In our online meetings, I could not see facial expressions or body language, so as I wrote fieldnotes and transcripts I relied on oral cues like pauses, inflection, volume, background noise, overlapping of comments, and contextual information to help me describe the speaker's tone, delivery, and content. Often I would return to the same piece of audio repeatedly, listening again and again in order to try to better translate an oral interaction into written language. These were my first analytical moves: to take what happened in an online, oral meeting and translate it into various forms of text, attempting to characterize tone, emotion, and meaning.

To support my organization and reading of the shared texts, I created a table of all writing from the focal year, noting either the title or description of the text as well as the genre. I used this table, and variations of it, repeatedly as I wrote about the texts group members shared. For example, because I was interested in how writing group members invented our own writing projects, I coded the texts by initiator (self, other), purpose (personal, professional, academic), genre, and intended audience (including the self). I used those various coded tables to consider patterns in what types of texts we shared, when different types of texts emerged, and audience and purpose.

In organizing the talk and textual data, I made several distinct analytical passes. In one, I aligned the fieldnotes, transcripts, and shared written texts from each meeting. This move allowed me to "locate language and modes in use within their scene, situation, and time frame" (Heath & Street, 2008, p. 127). Reading through all the texts associated with each meeting, in the order they were experienced, allowed me to re-create that meeting and analyze the patterns that emerged.

Emerson, Fretz, and Shaw (1995) also emphasize the significance of researchers treating the fieldnotes as a complete text, "reviewing, experiencing, and reexamining everything that has been written down, while self-consciously seeking to identify themes, patterns, and variations within this record" (p. 144). This emphasis on *reading* my data also resonates with me as a writer, and it was a central feature of my analysis. Reading across my fieldnotes and transcripts, as well as across group members' written texts, allowed me to analyze specifically for development, recurring themes, writing strategies, and the way we orally connected our inventive work across meetings and across texts.

USING NARRATIVE WRITING AS A MODE OF INQUIRY

My research moves were also informed by the growing tradition of narrative inquiry, which emphasizes narrative as a *mode* of inquiry (Clandinin & Connelly, 2000; Pagnucci, 2004; Schaafsma & Vinz, 2011). In their text *On Narrative Inquiry,* Schaafsma and Vinz (2011) advise taking moments from a study and writing them up as "narrative nuggets," which "might nudge you to question further, to tell other stories," often leading to "the beginning of the inquiry" (p. 3). They write that research grows out of the "telling, questioning, and rendering of narratives," where *narrating* "is to do more than 'give' an account or 'tell' a story" (p. 3). They describe narrative writing itself as a critical analytical tool, through which a researcher might attempt to "*(re)live* an experience" (p. 53).

Schaafsma and Vinz (2011) emphasize the significance of using narrative to show (rather than tell) what occurs in a research setting, drawing on moves often associated with creative nonfiction writing. They claim, "the verb *narrate* suggests shaping through strategies such as repetition, intensity, linkage, magnification, tensions, and/or interpretations," making the presence of the author visible "in the markings of the text and in the crafting and shaping of the experiences" (p. 3). In making these claims, they join other researchers who look to story as a tool for inquiry (Clandinin & Connelly, 2000; Pagnucci, 2004; Paley, 1989).

Drawing on this work in narrative inquiry played a critical role in my analysis. For example, as I wrote vignettes from the transcripts of Christina sharing each version of her "Identity Crisis" text, I was forced to attend closely to the flow of the conversation, the way different people spoke or responded, and the connection between the oral talk and the written text. Writing these narrative scenes required me to listen to audiotapes and revisit transcripts over and over again, as I tried to "(re)live" those moments from past meetings. In other narrative vignettes I wrote, I was pushed to characterize the nature of verbal exchanges, for example, the discomfort in Nell's voice as she talked about having to prepare a wedding toast and the ways Karen performed different students' voices when she told a story. Because I am still in the writing group with Karen, Jillian, Nell, and Christina, I have been able to share my drafts and analyses with them, to ask for their interpretations and feedback.

Indeed, this was a study where the line between the "inquiry" and the "writing it up" were often blurred (Emerson et al., 1995; Heath & Street, 2008; Schaafsma & Vinz, 2011). I was writing and inquiring throughout this project: as I wrote my own texts and shared these with fellow group members; as I wrote about what we discussed in my fieldnotes and transcripts; and as I wrote to explore patterns, consider inventive moves, compare experiences across meetings, and interrogate my interpretations. Using narrative throughout this book helped me bring our writing group to life, hopefully allowing readers to experience something of our meetings and witness moments of our inventions.

References

Atwell, N. (1998). *In the middle: New understandings about writing, reading, and learning.* Portsmouth, NH: Boynton/Cook.

Bitzer, L. (1995). The rhetorical situation. In W. A. Covino & D. A. Jolliffe (Eds.), *Rhetoric: Concepts, definitions, boundaries* (pp. 300–310). Boston, MA: Allyn & Bacon.

Blau, S. (1999). The only new thing under the sun: 25 years of the National Writing Project. *The Quarterly (of the National Writing Project), 21*(3). Retrieved from www.nwp.org/cs/public/print/resource/804.

Bogdan, R. C., & Biklen, S. K. (2007). *Qualitative research for education: An introduction to theories and methods.* Boston, MA: Pearson.

Bomer, K. (2005). *Writing a life: Teaching memoir to sharpen insight, shape meaning—and triumph over tests.* Portsmouth, NH: Heinemann.

Bridgford, K. (2001). Writing within a community. *The Voice, 6*(1), 20–21.

Brown, J. (2006). Fire. In *A leader's guide to reflective practice.* Bloomington, IN: Trafford.

Burroughs, R. (1995). Different strokes: Composing in a writing group. *The Quarterly (of the National Writing Project), 17*(2), 3–6.

Calkins, L. M. (1986). *The art of teaching writing.* Portsmouth, NH: Heinemann.

Check, J. (2002). Reflection and reform. *The Quarterly (of the National Writing Project), 24*(3).

Cisneros, S. (1987). *My wicked, wicked ways.* New York, NY: Turtle Bay.

Clandinin, D. J., & Connelly, F. M. (2000). *Narrative inquiry: Experience and story in qualitative research.* San Francisco, CA: Jossey-Bass

Dahl, K. L. (Ed.). (1992). *Teacher as writer: Entering the professional conversation.* Urbana, IL: National Council of Teachers of English.

Dawson, C. (2009). Beyond checklists and rubrics: Engaging students in authentic conversations about their writing. *English Journal, 98*(5), 66–71.

Dawson, C., Robinson, E., Hanson, K., VanRiper, J., & Ponzio, C. (2013). Creating a breathing space: An online teachers' writing group. *English Journal, 102*(3), 93–99.

Dobie, A. (2008). What to do after your summer vacation: Guides to starting your own writing group. *National Writing Project.* Retrieved from www.nwp.org/cs/public/print/resource/2695

Dunning, S., & Stafford, W. (1992). *Getting the Knack: 20 poetry writing exercises.* Urbana, IL: National Council of Teachers of English.

Durst, R. K. (1992). A writer's community: How teachers can form writing groups. In K. L. Dahl (Ed.), *Teacher as writer: Entering the professional conversation,* 261–271. Urbana, IL: National Council of Teachers of English.

Elbow, P. (1998). *Writing without teachers* (2nd ed.). New York, NY: Oxford University Press.

Elrod, A. (2003). Reflections on an online teachers writing group. *The Quarterly (of the National Writing Project), 25*(1), 21–29.

Emerson, R. M., Fretz, R. I., & Shaw, L. L. (1995). *Writing ethnographic fieldnotes.* Chicago, IL: University of Chicago Press.

Emig, J. (1971). *The composing processes of twelfth graders.* Urbana, IL: National Council of Teachers of English.

Fleischman, P. (2005). *Joyful noise: Poems for two voices.* New York: HarperCollins.

Fletcher, R. (1993). *What a writer needs.* Portsmouth, NH: Heinemann.

Fletcher, R., & Portalupi, J. (2001). *Writing workshop: The essential guide.* Portsmouth, NH: Heinemann.

Flythe, V. L. (1989). Beginning a faculty writing group. *English Journal, 78*(5), 62–63.

Gee, J. P. (1996). *Social linguistics and literacies: Ideology in discourses* (2nd ed.). Bristol, PA: Taylor & Francis.

Gere, A. R. (1980). Teachers as writers. *The National Writing Project Network Newsletter, 2*(2), 1–2.

Gillespie, T. (1985). Becoming your own expert—Teachers as writers. *The Quarterly (of the National Writing Project), 8*(1), 1–2.

Gillespie, T. (1991). Joining the debate: *Shouldn't* writing teachers write? *The Quarterly (of the National Writing Project), 13*(3), 3–6.

Gillespie, T. (1995). Revisited article: Joining the debate: *Shouldn't* writing teachers write? *The Quarterly (of the National Writing Project), 17*(1), 37–41.

Goldberg, N. (2005). *Writing down the bones: Freeing the writer within.* Boston, MA: Shambhala.

Grosskopf, D. (2004). Writing myself awake. *The Quarterly (of the National Writing Project), 26*(2). Retrieved from www.nwp.org/cs/public/print/resource/1789

Hansard, G., & Irglova, M. (2006). Drown out. On *The Swell Season* [CD]. Chicago, IL: Overcoat Recordings.

Hawhee, D. (2002). Kairotic encounters. In J. M. Atwill & J. M. Lauer (Eds.), *Perspectives on rhetorical invention,* 16–35. Knoxville: University of Tennessee Press.

Heard, G. (1989). *For the good of the earth and sun: Teaching poetry.* Portsmouth, NH: Heinemann.

Heard, G. (1995). *Writing toward home: Tales and lessons to find your way.* Portsmouth, NH: Heinemann.

Heath, S. B., & Street, B. (2008). *On ethnography.* New York, NY: Teachers College Press.

Hicks, T. (2013). *Crafting digital writing: Composing texts across media and genres.* Portsmouth, NH: Heinemann.

Hicks, T., Busch-Grabmeyer, E., Hyler, J., & Smoker, A. (2013). Write, respond, repeat: A model for teachers' professional writing groups in a digital age. In Pytash, K.E., Ferdig, R.E., & Rasinski, T.V. (Eds.), *Preparing teachers to teach writing using technology* (pp. 149–161). Pittsburgh, PA: ETC Press.

Hillocks, G. J. (1995). *Teaching writing as reflective practice.* New York, NY: Teachers College Press.

Jago, C. (2002). *Sandra Cisneros in the classroom: "Do not forget to reach."* Urbana, IL: National Council of Teachers of English.

Johnston, P. (2004). *Choice words: How our language affects children's learning.* Portland, ME: Stenhouse.

Jost, K. (1990). Rebuttal: Why high-school writing teachers should not write. *English Journal, 79*(3), 65–66.

Kittle, P. (2008). *Write beside them: Risk, voice, and clarity in high school writing.* Portsmouth, NH: Heinemann.

Lamott, A. (1995). *Bird by bird: Some instructions on writing and life.* New York, NY: Doubleday.

LeFevre, K. B. (1987). *Invention as a social act.* Carbondale: Southern Illinois University Press.

McEntee, G. H. (1998). Diving with whales: Five reasons for practitioners to write for publication. *The Quarterly (of the National Writing Project), 20*(4), 21–26.

Morris, C., & Haight, D. K. (1993). A funny thing happened when we began to write. *English Journal, 82(8),* 25–29.

Murray, D. M. (1968). *A writer teaches writing: A practical method of teaching composition.* Boston, MA: Houghton Mifflin.

Murray, D. M. (1996). *Crafting a life in essay, story, poem.* Portsmouth, NH: Boynton/Cook.

Nelms, B. (1990). Editor's note to rebuttal: Why writing teachers should—or should not—write. *English Journal, 79*(9), 25.

Pagnucci, G. S. (2004). *Living the narrative life: Stories as a tool for meaning making.* Portsmouth, NH: Heinemann.

Paley, V. G. (1989). *Must teachers also be writers?* (Occasional Paper No. 13). Berkeley, CA: Center for the Study of Writing.

Perry, R. (1995). The temptations of tobacco and other stories: Reaching students through modeling. *The Quarterly (of the National Writing Project), 17*(14), 12–15.

Prior, P. (2004). Tracing process: How texts come into being. In C. Bazerman & P. Prior (Eds.), *What writing does and how it does it: An introduction to analyzing texts and textual practices* (pp. 167–200). Mahwah, NJ: Lawrence Erlbaums.

Ray, K. W. (2006). *Study driven: A framework for planning units of study in the writing workshop.* Portsmouth, NH: Heinemann.

Ray, K. W., with Laminack, L. L. (2001). *The writing workshop: Working through the hard parts (and they're all hard parts).* Urbana, IL: National Council of Teachers of English.

Robbins, S., Seaman, G., Yancey, K. B., & Yow, D. (Eds.). (2006). *Teachers' writing groups: Collaborative inquiry and reflection for professional growth.* Kennesaw, GA: Kennesaw State University Press.

Rosenthal, L. (Ed.). (2003). *The writing group book: Creating and sustaining a successful writing group.* Chicago, IL: Chicago Review Press.

Schaafsma, D., & Vinz, R. (2011). *On narrative inquiry.* New York, NY: Teachers College Press.

Simone, F. (1995). Wrestling with an alien craft. *The Quarterly (of the National Writing Project), 17*(2), 1–2.

Smagorinsky, P., Johannessen, L.R., Kahn, E.A., & McCann, T.M. (2010). *The dynamics of writing instruction: A structured process approach for middle and high school.* Portsmouth, NH: Heinemann.

Whitney, A. E. (2008). Teacher transformation in the National Writing Project. *Research in the Teaching of English, 43*(2), 144–187.

Whitney, A. E. (2009). Writer, teacher, person: Tensions between personal and professional writing in a National Writing Project Summer Institute. *English Education, 41*(3), 235–258.

Whitney, A. E. (2013, September 23). And yet we write: Being a teacher-writer [Blog post]. Retrieved from writerswhocare.wordpress.com/2013/09/23/and-yet-we-write-being-a-teacher-writer/

Whitney, A. E., Anderson, K., Dawson, C., Kang, S., Olan Rios, E., Olcese, N., & Ridgeman, M. (2012). Audience and authority in the professional writing of teacher-authors. *Research in the Teaching of English, 46*(4), 390–419.

Whitney, A.E., Hicks, T., Zuidema, L., Fredricksen, J.E., & Yagelski, R.P. (2014). Teacher-writers: Then, now, and next. *Research in the Teaching of English, 49*(2), 177–184.

Williams, T. (1990). The gift of writing groups. *English Journal, 79*(4), 58–60.

Yagelski, R. P. (2009). A thousand writers writing: Seeking change through the radical practice of writing as a way of being. *English Education, 42*(1), 6–28.

Yagelski, R. P. (2011). *Writing as a way of being: Writing instruction, nonduality, and the crisis of sustainability.* New York, NY: Hampton Press.

Yagelski, R. P. (2012). Writing as praxis. *English Education, 44*(2), 188–204.

Index

"Abuelito Who" (Cisneros), 88
Anderson, K., 1, 7, 92
"Angela" letter (Christine), 37, 77,
    83–86, 125
Atwell, N., 5, 19, 121
Audio/video conferencing. *See* Technical
    issues for online writing groups

"Barriers" vignettes (Christina), 52,
    55–56, 126
Biklen, S. K., 18
Bird by Bird (Lamott), 95
Bitzer, L., 77–78
Blau, Sheridan, 7, 8
Blogging, 22, 28, 32, 34, 43–45, 56,
    107
Bogdan, R. C., 18
Bomer, K., 121
Brainstorming, 24, 31, 34, 55, 63, 68,
    79, 126
Bridgford, K., 9
Brown, Judy, 12, 114
Burroughs, Robert, 9
Busch-Grabmeyer, E., 1, 9, 25

Calkins, L. M., 5
Character sketches, 61–62, 73, 126
Check, J., 92
Christina (teacher-writer)
    "Barriers" vignettes, 52, 55–56, 126
    blogging by, 22, 32, 34, 43–45, 56,
        107
    cookbook introduction, 73–74, 126
    described, 15–16
    as ESL instructor/coordinator, 15,
        35–36, 45, 77, 80–83, 126
    "Foreign" (school poem), 125
    "Identity Crisis/The Battle" (poem/

narrative), 43, 64, 74, 95, 98,
    106–111, 120, 125–126
    mother timeline, 35, 125
    presentation notes/Title III meeting,
        35–36, 45, 77, 80–83, 126
    reasons for joining teacher-writer
        group, 15
    reflections on writing group, 113–
        114
    school newsletter, 126
    table of written texts in focal year,
        125–126
    Twitter writing, 52, 53, 55–56
Christine (teacher-writer). *See also*
    Dawson, Christine; Methodology
    of study
    "Angela" letter, 37, 77, 83–86, 125
    Christmas poem, 125
    described, 16–17
    found language/poem from aunt's
        emails, 58–61, 63, 119–120, 126
    gardening essay, 64, 126
    oral brainstorming/essay, 79
    poem on fantasy books, 17, 125
    reasons for joining teacher-writer
        group, 12, 16–17
    table of written texts in focal year,
        125–126
    teacher-mentor role, 13–14, 17–18
    teaching award essay, 69–70, 125
Cisneros, Sandra, 88, 89
Clandinin, D. J., 127, 129
Cloud storage, 21–22, 26, 28
"A Comfortable Hell" poem (Nell),
    34–35, 46, 125
Composing identities, 95–112
    expanding notions of teacher-
        writers, 98

135

About the Author

Christine M. Dawson is a writer, teacher educator, and writing research- er. She is on the leadership team for the Capital District Writing Project (a site of the National Writing Project), and she teaches curriculum stud- ies and literacy courses to preservice teachers at the college level. Christine earned her doctorate in Curriculum, Instruction, and Teacher Education from Michigan State University, and she holds an MA in Curriculum and Teaching from Columbia University Teachers College and a BA from the University of Virginia. Prior to pursuing her doctorate, Christine taught sec- ondary English for 10 years, served as an English department coordinator for a middle/high school, and was a literacy coach. She has been award- ed several teaching awards, including Michigan State University College of Education's Excellence and Innovation in Teaching Award and New Jersey's Middlesex County Teacher of the Year Award. Her research interests focus on writing studies and pedagogies, teacher education, curriculum design, and the significance of teachers' own writing on their beliefs and pedagog- ical practices. She presents regularly at national and international confer- ences, and her scholarly writing has been published in *English Journal* and *Research in the Teaching of English*. She also had the opportunity to work with Arthur Applebee and Judith Langer on the National Study of Writing Instruction, and she is a coauthor with them of *Writing Instruction That Works: Proven Methods for Middle and High School Classrooms* (Teachers College Press, 2013). She may be reached at dawson23@gmail.com or www.christinedawson.net.